To our family

For your encouragement and support in all our endeavours

The Making of Liverpool

Portraits of a City by

The Singh Twins

The Making of Liverpool:

Portraits of a City by The Singh Twins

 Published by Twin Studio
twinstudio@hotmail.com

First edition 2010
Copyright © The Singh Twins, March 2010
www.singhtwins.co.uk

ISBN 978-0-9535111-2-9

Designed by The Singh Twins
Printed in Spain

Supported by

Contents

Acknowledgements

We are most grateful to Liverpool City Council, Merseytravel, Milap Festival Trust and the Northwest Regional Development Agency (NWDA) for their kind support in funding this publication.

With special thanks also to:

BBC Radio Merseyside Producer, Angela Heslop, for allowing us to use her interview with us in this publication.

Fellow artists Mark McGann, Steve Mason and the team at Sparkle Media (Andy Cooper, Tom Crate, Heidi Duff, Neil Parsons and Mike Snowdon) for their creative contribution and dedication to the 'The Making of Liverpool' animation and for supplying imagery for this book.

Guy Woodland and Judy Tasker for their invaluable assistance with the production and proofreading of this publication.

Colin Hunt for his help in researching images from the Liverpool Echo and Daily Post archive.

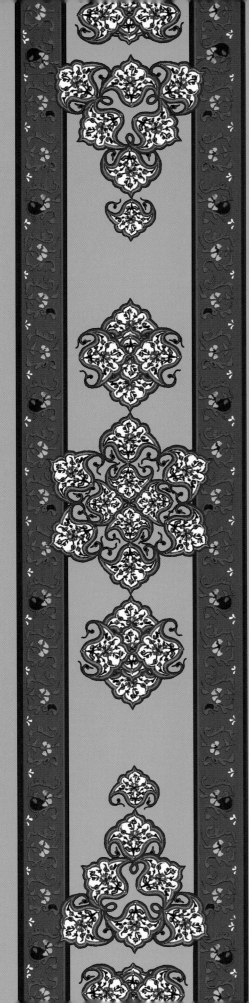

Forewords

Page 16   www.liverpoolecho.co.uk   ****   Liverpool *ECHO*

O8 DAYS A WEEK
THE ECHO'S DAILY CULTURE PAGE

Art shows our pool of talent

By CATHERINE JONES
Culture Reporter

Singh twins draw on city's cultural depth

AN INTRICATE painting celebrating the best of Liverpool culture took its artists two years to create.

The award-winning Singh Twins have incorporated everything from community arts groups to the city's big theatres and Sir Simon Rattle in the Art Matters: Pool of Life painting commissioned by Liverpool Cultures Company.

The Wirral-based artists said they wanted to encapsulate all facets of the city's wide-ranging cultural scene.

Their painting, which will hang in the Bluecoat throughout 2008, also includes Ken Dodd, Pete Postlethwaite, Cilla Black, Steven Gerrard and Adrian Henri.

Amrit Singh said: 'Our main focus was the community groups, arts organisations and individuals that have grafted over the years to make Liverpool the cultural centre it is today.

'We've tried to represent a cross-section of what culture is all about, alongside familiar figures which represent the world of sport and the arts.'

Her sister, Rabindra, added: 'The theme is very theatrical. The figures on the balconies for example are people from various different paintings that are going

to be shown in 2008.'

Culture Company executive producer Fiona Gasper said: "This painting is a fantastic interpretation of Liverpool's European Capital of Culture year, and will serve as a permanent legacy to the city's celebrations.'

Art Matters: Pool of Life is the second of two works commissioned from the Singh Twins by the Culture Company.

The first, marking Liverpool's 800th Birthday, was unveiled by Prince Charles at St George's Hall last April.

The twins also have arts council funding for an animation explaining the coat-of-arms inspired Liverpool 800: The Changing Face of Liverpool in detail.

The short film is narrated by Mark McGann, and a new song has been composed by American singer-songwriter Harps, who came to Liverpool to record the track.

The 15-minute animation will be shown at film festivals in the US and Canada, and the twins hope it will eventually be screened next to the painting in St George's Hall.

TWIN POWERS: Rabindra, left, and Amrit Singh, with their Capital of Culture artwork Art Matters: The Pool of Life at the newly-reopened Bluecoat

Top. The Singh Twins showing HRH Prince Charles 'Liverpool 800: The Changing Face of Liverpool' (commissioned by Liverpool City Council for the city's 800th birthday) on the occasion of its official unveiling at Liverpool St George's Hall.
Middle. Liverpool Echo feature about The Singh Twins' European Capital of Culture commission, 'Arts Matters: The Pool of Life'.
Bottom. The Singh Twins receiving their Honorary Citizenship of Liverpool from the Lord Mayor of Liverpool, Councillor Steve Rotheram.

The past decade has seen a wonderful flowering of creative talent across Liverpool and Merseyside. And, thanks to being European Capital of Culture 2008, it's been pleasing to see many artists gaining national and international attention.

Of course, some artists have been international cultural ambassadors long before 2008 and that description certainly applies to Amrit and Rabindra Singh.

When the city council was looking to celebrate the twin peaks of the city's 800th birthday and Capital of Culture, we wanted to capture the global feel of the city through new works of art. Who better for Liverpool to commission than artists whose very work is a perfect blend of East meets West.

I know personally how much time and effort The Singh Twins put into their art and their two city commissions perfectly captured the zeitgeist, while reflecting an age-old process that is both an education and inspiration.

Their rise to prominence both here and abroad, where they are causing a renaissance of their style, have also made them fantastic role models. So much so that they were quite rightly awarded the status of Honorary Citizens of Liverpool last year.

Indeed, such is their unique approach I was delighted to hear that they have found the time to put their fascinating work into this book.

I'm sure any art lover will find much to discover and learn and the city council is only too delighted to support The Singh Twins in this venture.

I hope it brings a new audience and a new way of looking and appreciating both them and the vibrant culture that flourishes in this city region. Enjoy the read and journey.

Councillor Warren Bradley
Leader, Liverpool City Council

Warren Bradley

England's Northwest is one of the most culturally diverse and vibrant regions of the UK. Talented artists such as Amrit and Rabindra have contributed so much to the vibrancy of the region, so it's always inspiring to engage with their work.

I first came across them when they had a big show at the Walker Art Gallery in Liverpool in 2005 and I was struck by the powerful political and social themes presented in the beautifully decorative and traditional Indian miniature painting style they use. So I had no hesitation accepting an invitation to their studio to talk about a new project, which has led to the production of this marvellous book.

The city of Liverpool has undergone a huge transformation over the last decade to become a true European capital, with a healthy tourism industry and a dynamic cultural scene at its heart. The Singh Twins' work offers a personal expression of the pride both artists have in this, their home city, and the Northwest region they have grown up, been educated and now work in.

This book shows the Northwest at its best; showcasing Liverpool as a vibrant city of academic excellence, culture, commerce, tourism and leisure. It's a true inspiration and a fascinating insight into the effect that a place can have on art and I'm privileged to have had the opportunity to work with them on it.

Peter Mearns
Executive Director of Marketing and Communications
Northwest Regional Development Agency (NWDA)

Milap Festival Trust is an innovative, dynamic, professional Indian arts organisation based in Liverpool, the Music City of Britain, with a body of pioneering work that stretches back to 1985.

We are a registered charity devoted to promoting and popularising all aspects of Indian arts through a wide-ranging, country-wide, year-round programme of education, promotions, commissions and community events, which aim to bring together people of all communities, and create fresh cultural collaborations that transcend the barriers of language, race, religion and diverse cultural traditions.

As part of the new initiatives the Trust has launched, we conceived and created SAMYO, the first ever South Asian Music Youth Orchestra and, later, TARANG the national Indian classical music ensemble. Both of these orchestras are now nationally recognised and provide education, training and performance opportunities for young people to help them evolve into professional musicians. We also run two very popular summer schools: Dance India and Music India and commission new dance and music programmes for major theatres in Manchester, London and Liverpool.

The essential focus of the Trust is to be the dynamic, driving force for Indian arts nationally and internationally, working to achieve excellence in all that we undertake.

We are delighted to be involved in a project which showcases the presence of Indian arts in Liverpool and Britain through the work of two very talented and established international artists who have brought pride to Liverpool. As a leading Indian Arts Festival in Britain, we are always keen to present the very best in Indian arts practice and it is, therefore, a great pleasure to be able to support the production of this excellent book that celebrates the best of our home city of Liverpool, especially in this our 25th anniversary year.

Prashant Nayak
Executive Director, Milap Festival Trust

The Singh Twins' unique talent for showcasing and promoting the Liverpool City Region in such a lively and exciting way is a true gift, expressing the rich cultural heritage that Liverpool City Region holds. Merseytravel, co-ordinating integrated transport across the region are great supporters of our cultural heritage and showing the rest of the world what an exciting destination the Liverpool City Region is. Our Public Art Strategy aims to help all travellers enjoy their journey experience via 'Art on the Network,' striving for a surprise at every corner.

These surprises now incorporate The Singh Twins' work on our premises, including some special showings of their delightful animation 'The Making of Liverpool,' for passengers to enjoy as they travel through some of our interchanges, whatever their journey's purpose. We know our passengers have embraced 'Art on the Network,' by their response to our open competition to provide some art for their own community and are thrilled that The Singh Twins have agreed to be our judges for the competition. We congratulate The Singh Twins on their ability to capture the spirit of Liverpool in their vibrant work – long may it continue!

Neil Scales OBE
Chief Executive and Director General
Merseytravel

Left. 'Mary and Child'. The Singh Twins, 1995.

Introduction

Above. An early mural of the founder of Sikhism, Guru Nanak (from Baba Atal Gurdwara, Amritsar), painted in a tradtion of the Indian miniature style which has influenced The Singh Twin's work.

The Singh Twins, Amrit and Rabindra, are London-born sisters of Indian origin who grew up in the Northwest region of England, very much isolated from the wider British Asian community but as part of a traditional Indian extended family. Although Sikhs by birth, they underwent a Catholic convent education, which had a lasting impact on their lives and established their early interest in the rich symbolism of religious iconography and art. As teenagers they visited India for the first time, in 1980, and returned to England with a renewed passion, deeper understanding and greater affiliation for their traditional Indian heritage. It was an experience that would come to define their own sense of identity as British Asians and shape the development of the personal creative style for which they are known.

Although appreciating and creating art since as far back as they can remember, the Twins at that time and up till the mid-80s had no desire to be professional artists but decided instead on a career in academia. Pursuing their longstanding fascination for world religions and mythologies they initially read for a Liverpool University BA (Hons) Combined Studies degree in Comparative Religion, Ecclesiastical History and 20th Century Western Art History, and later Religion and the Arts at Manchester University. Whilst at Manchester, they went on to specialise in Sikh art and iconography at postgraduate level and won an INTACH scholarship to carry out a year's field research in India.

Their ultimate decision to reject a career in academia in favour of one in art was largely a response to the negative attitudes they received from university tutors over the personal styles they had begun to develop as part of the practical module of their Western Art History course – styles which were rooted in the centuries-old tradition of Indian miniature painting.

Left. Traditional Indian miniature painting. 'Jujhar Singh Bundela Kneels in Submission to Shah Jahan'. By Bichitr, with details by Harif, c1630. ©The Trustees of the Chester Beatty Library, Dublin.

Above left and right. Early studies of Indian miniature painting. The Singh Twins, 1980.

*Left.*Traditional Indian miniature painting. 'Dara Shikoh with Sages in a Garden', c1640–50. ©The Trustees of the Chester Beatty Library, Dublin.

Above. Three of The Singh Twins' early studies of Indian miniature painting, inspired by 'Dara Shikoh with Sages in a Garden'.

In spite of being frustrated by their tutors' dismissal of the Indian miniature tradition and the pressure put on them to look instead to western role models for inspiration, the Twins initially tried to comply with the expectations of their art department without compromising their own artistic preferences and turned to movements and artists within western art which they had admired long before they discovered the Indian miniature; namely the Pre-Raphaelites, Art Nouveau and illustrators like William Blake, William Morris and Aubrey Beardsley. However, it was made clear to them that within the context of contemporary art development their natural inclination towards the decorative, illustrative and romantic in western art was also unacceptable.

Left. Winter and Autumn. The Singh Twins, 1987.
Right. Illustration to Edgar Allan Poe.
The Singh Twins, 1996.
Inspired by Aubrey Beardsley.

Although demoralised by the lack of support and respect for the choices they made in developing their artistic self-expression, the experience demonstrated to the Twins just how important art was both as an embodiment of cultural ideals and values and a tool for communication. Instead of bending to what they regarded as the institutionalised prejudice of the art establishment, they decided to challenge the system by returning to the Indian miniature and championing its modern development on an international platform.

Left. 'Lady in Pink'. The Singh Twins, 1985.
Inspired by Alphonse Mucha.
Right. 'Daddy in the Sitting Room III'. The Singh Twins, 1987.
A modern reworking of the Indian miniature style.

Above. 'Tribute to Cha-cha Baldave: Forever in Our Hearts'. The Singh Twins, 1995. A painting which, in style draws on Egyptian, Indian, Persian, Chinese and Renaissance art and incorporates Hindu, Christian, Buddhist, Sikh and Islamic iconography.
Right. A composite of details from The Twins' work that reference various sources.
Below. Examples of global symbolic imagery used in other works by The Singh Twins.

Whilst their devotion to the miniature painting style has remained resolute, their art has become increasingly eclectic over the years, as the Twins continue to combine their love of this distinct tradition within Indian art with an equal interest in the rich symbolism and traditional aesthetics of different cultures globally.

The Liverpool Connection

Within the range of themes they have explored throughout their career, the Twins' home city of Liverpool and the Northwest of England, where they have lived, studied and worked most of their lives, have been significant sources of pride and inspiration to them.

Their creative relationship with Liverpool began in 1994 when its oldest art centre, the Bluecoat, offered the Twins their first public gallery show. Since then they have represented Liverpool at home and abroad, as exhibiting artists and speakers at international art exchanges, seminars, festivals and cultural celebrations. In 1996 the then Museum of Liverpool Life purchased their first Singh Twins painting, 'O Come All Ye Re-eds', which was on public display until 2006 when the museum closed and it was placed in the archives.

Left. A composite of details referencing Liverpool from works by The Singh Twins.

The same work was later selected by the national gallery of the north, (the Liverpool Walker Art Gallery) for inclusion in 'The Rise of Women Artists' – an exhibition of works from National Museums Liverpool's permanent collections that "represent some of history's most celebrated female artists". When Liverpool's multi-million pound flagship centre for film, art and creative technology (FACT) opened in 2003 it incorporated new works especially commissioned from the Twins – a series of symbolic portraits profiling key people associated with the building, installed as light boxes.

Besides creating and promoting their own work, the Twins have also played an active role in helping to enrich the cultural life of Liverpool and the Northwest by curating exhibitions and cultural programmes, such as the 'Zindabad Festival of Indian Art' in 1997, 'Festival of Punjab Art' in 1999 and 'Sikhs in Print' in 2008, which showcase diverse arts and aim to cultivate greater intercultural understanding.

In 2005 the Walker Art Gallery hosted 'Past Modern', one of the most successful solo retrospectives of the Twins' work and, in 2008, the sisters became the first recipients of the Liverpool Art Prize, People's Choice Award. In 2009 their artistic contribution to the city was officially recognised when they were conferred with the status of Honorary Citizens of Liverpool.

Right. 'The FACT Portraits' commission. The Singh Twins, 2002.

Amongst The Singh Twins' most significant and well-known Liverpool-inspired works are two paintings commissioned by Liverpool City Council to mark the 800th birthday celebrations of the city in 2007 and its status as European Capital of Culture in 2008 (entitled, 'Liverpool 800: The Changing Face of Liverpool' and 'Arts Matters: The Pool of Life'), and an award-winning Arts Council England-funded animation entitled 'The Making of Liverpool'.

Both the paintings and the animation clearly reflect the Twins' passion and fascination for their home city and are described by them as being:

"the most challenging, ambitious and comprehensive representations of Liverpool we have worked on".

Right. Detail from the 'Arts Matters: The Pool of Life' drawing. The Singh Twins, 2008.

Arts Matters:
the pool of life

'Arts Matters' celebrates Liverpool's status as European Capital of Culture in 2008. Taking almost a year to research and complete, it captures the aspirations and spirit of the occasion and reflects the city's rich and lively cultural life. Included in the composition are the two official 08 opening ceremonies and many of the events programmed, not only by Liverpool's main arts venues, but by individuals and community groups whose contribution at grassroots level has remained the backbone of the city's cultural and artistic creativity. Like all of The Singh Twins' work, symbolic content and composition convey a complex narrative about the subject. The theatrical theme presents Liverpool as a world-class stage at the "centre of the creative universe", rising from the River Mersey, upon which the very best in arts, culture and diversity is showcased. Dominating the stage are three female figures, which reinterpret Raphael's 'The Three Graces'. They symbolise the famous architectural 'Three Graces' of Liverpool's waterfront, namely the Liver, Cunard and Port of Liverpool Buildings. Together they hold up what has been dubbed Liverpool's 'Fourth Grace' (the New Museum of Liverpool). The Liver, Cunard and Port of Liverpool Buildings, (symbols of the city's past identity as a maritime, merchant city) are subservient to and smaller in size than the New Liverpool Museum, as Liverpool's past image gives way to its new identity as a city of tourism, leisure and culture. A fact which is further represented by the attire of each of 'The Three Graces', which is made up of imagery representing Performance Art, Visual Art and Sport. Within the scene are some well known figures connected with Liverpool – including Steven Gerrard, Yoko Ono, Adrian Henri, Holly Johnson, Pete Postlethwaite, Sir Simon Rattle, Ken Dodd, Cilla Black, and The Singh Twins themselves. Hailing from the worlds of TV, Film, Literature, Art, Comedy, Music and Sport, they collectively denote the rich creative talent of the Liverpool area past and present. Arriving at the harbour in a Tall Ship, they are

the 'precious cargo' of art and culture, which has come to replace the traditional cargo of Liverpool's trading past. The cityscape is made up of buildings from Liverpool, its twin city of Shanghai and other European port cities linked with the 2008 celebrations, namely: Marseilles, Naples, Bremen, Gdansk, Istanbul and Stavanger. The globe supporting St George's Hall symbolises the idea of 'The World in One City', whilst the sky of day and night together mark the continuous programme of celebration which took place throughout the European Capital of Culture Year. The impact of 08 on the city's regeneration is symbolised by the newly developed waterfront, depicted just below the cityscape (top right). Media interest in the celebration is represented by the film crew and photographer who mingle with the spectators, the Radio City text on the BMX ramp and the Radio City tower. Key sponsors of the event (the BBC and Liverpool Echo) are also referenced. Overseas visitor participation in 08 is also alluded to by the spectator crowd (bottom left), which includes portraits of some of the artists' friends and family who live abroad.

Right. 'Arts Matters: The Pool of Life'. The Singh Twins, 2008.
Above and near right. Details from 'Arts Matters'.

Left and above. Working processes for 'Arts Matters', showing a selection of photographic and archive source material as well as tracings of some of the details used in the painting.

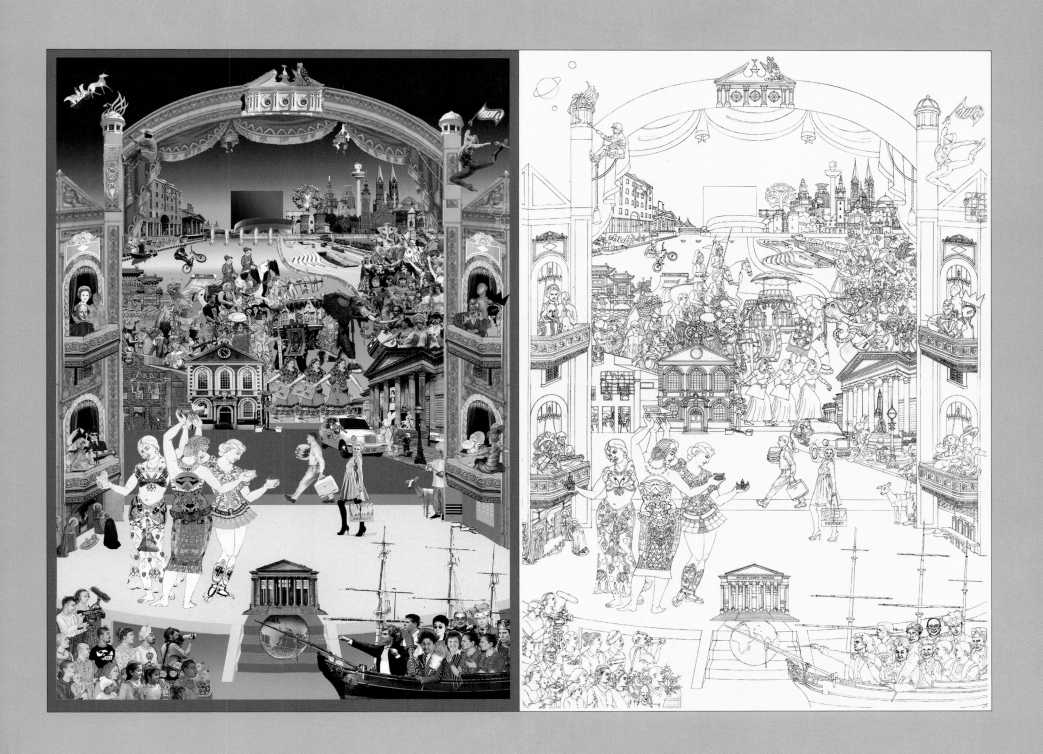

Above left. A computer-generated mock-up of the composition, incorporating web and
digitally scanned imagery, which was projected on to the canvas as a guide for the
production of the final drawing (*right*) for 'Arts Matters'.

Working processes for 'The Three Graces ' detail from 'Arts Matters', showing the initial simple line drawing (*above top*), the digital reworking of this (*left*), the detailed drawing (*above*) and the final painted version (*right*).

Left, this page and overleaf. Details from 'Arts Matters'.

Liverpool 800:
the changing
face of liverpool

'Liverpool 800' narrates the story of Liverpool through a symbolic depiction of the key historical periods and events that have helped to shape both its traditional identity as a Maritime Mercantile City and its modern identity as the European Capital of Culture. Commissioned to mark the city's 800th birthday in 2007, the painting is also a celebration of some of Liverpool's many achievements, its culturally diverse community and its rich heritage.

Left. 'Liverpool 800: The Changing Face of Liverpool'. The Singh Twins, 2007.
Above. Computer mock-up of the artists' reworking of Liverpool's coat of arms.

The main focus of the composition is a heraldic representation of Liverpool in which the city's traditional coat of arms - with its maritime associations - has been modified to reflect all aspects of the cultural identity it seeks to project today. Nevertheless, the fundamental components (ie the Shield, the Supporters, Neptune (left) and Triton (right) holding a staff, the motto etc) and style have been maintained, making the original coat of arms still recognisable - thus symbolising a celebration of Liverpool in the present whilst at the same time continuing to value and acknowledge the legacy of its past.

As with 'Arts Matters', 'Liverpool 800' was composed in part with the aid of a computer using imagery researched from different sources, including books, printed memorabilia and the internet. These rough layouts or mock-ups formed the basis of some sections of the detailed drawing (*right*).

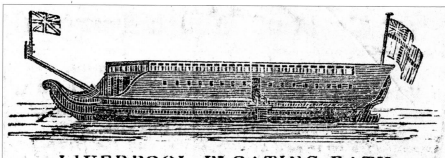

LIVERPOOL FLOATING BATH.

THE Public are respectfully informed that the FLOATING BATH is moored opposite the PRINCE'S PARADE, and is open for the reception of Company from Six o'Clock every morning until dusk.

Admittance, EIGHTPENCE each.

For Boys under Sixteen Years of Age, SIXPENCE each.

And on Sundays, for all Visitors SIXPENCE each.

Tickets for the season £1. each; for the month 9s.— Ditto for Boys under Twelve Years of Age 17s; Ditto for the month 7s.—To be had on board the Bath, or at T. Coglan's Office, 12, Exchange-street East.

Boats belonging to the Bath will be found at the Steps of the Parade, nearly opposite the Bath.

Left and right. Some of the different visual sources used in the 'Liverpool 800' painting (including an early version of the Liverpool coat of arms, a postcard commemorating Liverpool's 700th anniversary, a painting of the Cunard paddle steamer Britannia, an advert for Liverpool's floating bath and the Liverpool Dogs' Home and Speke airport's opening souvenir programme).

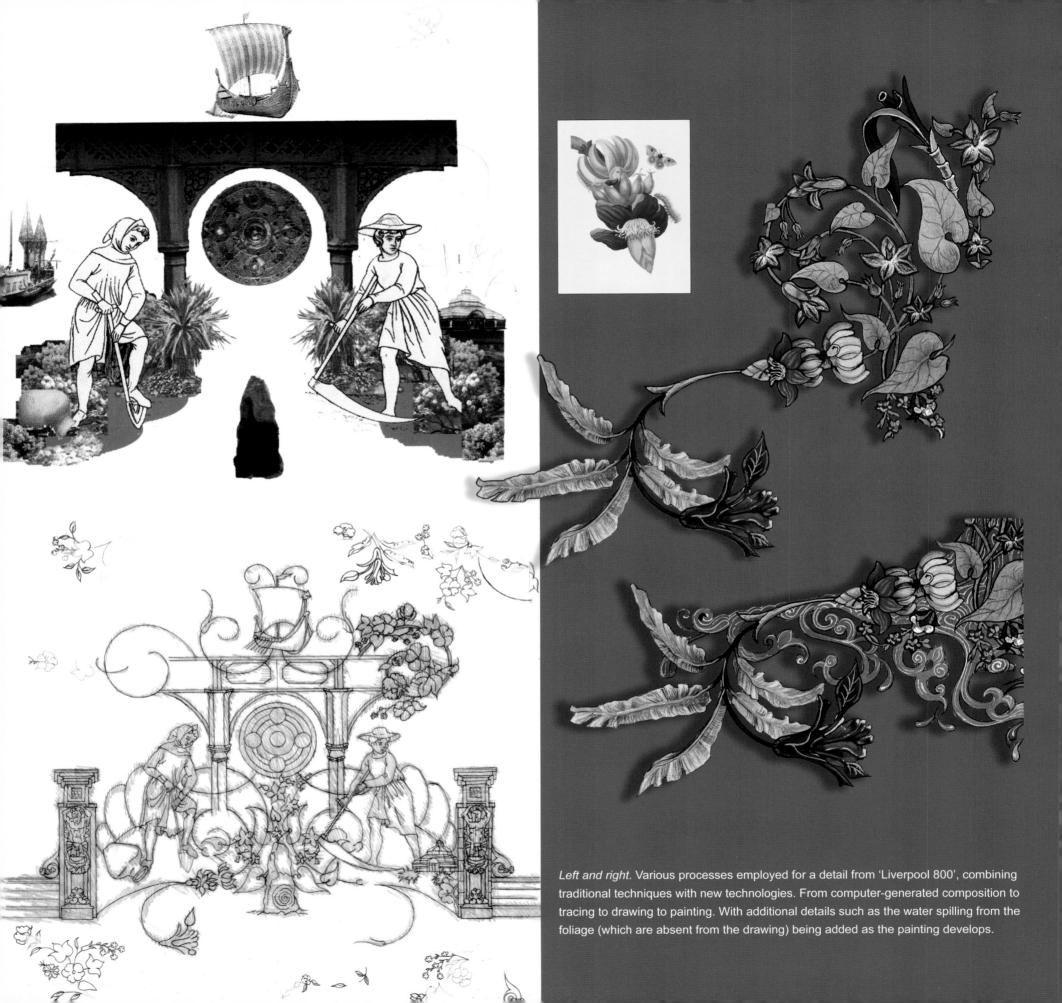

Left and right. Various processes employed for a detail from 'Liverpool 800', combining traditional techniques with new technologies. From computer-generated composition to tracing to drawing to painting. With additional details such as the water spilling from the foliage (which are absent from the drawing) being added as the painting develops.

Overleaf. Showing different stages in the painting process for this same detail.

Left. The completed section. *Above and overleaf*. Other details from 'Liverpool 800'.

Detail from 'Liverpool 800'.

50

Liverpool 800:
a city revealed

Ancient City

The gateway to Liverpool's largest public recreation area, Calderstones Park, with one of the ancient megaliths ('Calderstones') discovered there. Together these symbolise the prehistoric origins of settlement in the Liverpool area. The gateway itself also serves as the visual entry point into the story told by the painting.

The Viking ship symbolises Liverpool's settlement by the Vikings and Normans. 'Aigburth' and 'Aintree', seen adorning the ship's sails, are just two of the many Scandinavian-derived place names to be found in the Liverpool area that are evidence of this fact.

An axe and arrowhead represent the Bronze Age tools found in several Liverpool areas.

Birkenhead Priory, the oldest standing building in Merseyside. Situated on the Wirral peninsula, it was from here that the first known ferry across the River Mersey to Liverpool (and, in fact, the oldest recorded ferry in Britain) was operated by the Benedictine monks in the 1150s – a vital factor which greatly contributed to the opening up of Liverpool to settlers and its subsequent development as a trading port.

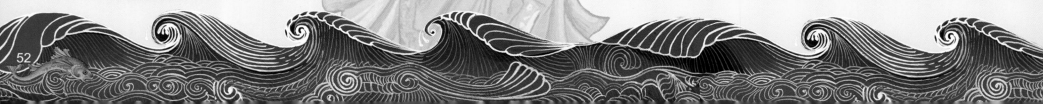

Holding a fishing net and scythe respectively, this couple symbolises the development of Liverpool into a small farming and fishing settlement during Medieval times.

The 'Kingston Brooch', believed to be the largest and finest example of its kind ever found, is in the collection of the Liverpool World Museum. It symbolises the Anglo-Saxon presence in the Liverpool area - as do the names 'Garston' and 'Walton' (two Liverpool areas of Anglo-Saxon origin), which have been incorporated into its decoration by the artists.

A hoard of Roman coins found in an urn in Liverpool's Toxteth Park represents the Roman presence in Liverpool.

St Nicholas' Church, whose origins go back to the 13th century, has always been a significant landmark, being one of the three original buildings (along with the Tower of Liverpool and Liverpool Castle) that can be seen in the earliest depictions of the city.

Maritime Mercantile City

This Tall Ship symbolises Liverpool's past role as a mercantile port city. The city's early trading activities as a provincial port from 1229 to the mid-1700s are symbolised by the ship's cargo:

- The Quaker represents the export of religious immigrants (Puritans, Protestants, Roman Catholics and Quakers) to the USA in Liverpool ships – a fact which greatly enhanced the development of trade with America.

- Bright coloured sails represent the export of dyed cottons from Kendal to Ireland.

- The ship's middle sail symbolises the fact that the first 'word cross', or crossword, was a Liverpool export to America (written by Scouser Arthur Wynne and carried by the 'New York World' newspaper in 1913.

- During the reign of Elizabeth I 'Liverpool [was] the most frequented passage to Ireland' and, given Liverpool's strategic position, the Tudor Queen commandeered its fleet to transport her troops there.

- The bobbin represents yarn, imported from Ireland.

- Animals and the shamrock represent the import of sheep, cattle and deer skin from Ireland.

- Sacks of coal represent the export of this fuel to Ireland.

- The Falk Salt packet represents the export of salt from England to Ireland, Newfoundland and the Mediterranean.

- Tate & Lyle sugar bags represent the export of sugar to Ireland.

- Stockings hanging on the bowsprit represent the export of coarse stockings from Sheffield to Ireland.

- Fish caught in a net represent herring, imported from Scotland.

Based on a painting of a Liverpool slave ship (William Jackson) in the Liverpool Maritime Museum, the Tall Ship also serves as a symbol of the city's involvement in 'the profitable but immoral Triangular Trade' from the mid 17th to early 19th century – an involvement which ultimately resulted in the city becoming the 'most important centre in the world for the organisation of the Slave Trade' and the largest and wealthiest city in England.

Cotton, banana, tobacco, cocoa and sugar cane – all commodities transported by Liverpool ships, during the Slave Trade – are represented by the plants at the bottom of the painting.

The Statue of Liberty represents Liverpool's strong historical and ongoing trade and migration links with the 'New World'.

The placement of the Liverpool cityscape between the Statue of Liberty and a Chinese Pagoda symbolises the dominance of the port in overseas trade, which extended to the farthest lands to both east and west. 'By 1850 more overseas trade was carried out at Liverpool than in any other city in the world'.

Liverpool's trade links with the Far East were established by the Blue Funnel Line in 1865.

City of Power

A detail borrowed from a postcard produced in commemoration of the 700th anniversary of the city depicts the granting of the charter by King John to the Steward of West Derby in 1207, whereby Liverpool was established as a Royal Borough. The scene's placement in the middle of the Mersey symbolises the vital importance this river and the activities relating to it had in the shaping of Liverpool as one of the most powerful trading cities in the world. The backdrop to the figures is the alchemical sign for earth, which is composed of two elements – a triangle, signifying earth, and a horizontal line, signifying water, which cuts across its apex. Representing stagnant water, which eventually solidifies into matter, this sign symbolises Liverpool's development from what was once mostly swamp land and the Pool, a tidal inlet which ran from Canning Place to Whitechapel.

Liverpool Castle – the biggest and most important building in the city for nearly 300 years – symbolises the early use of Liverpool as a Royal power base and military stronghold by King John and subsequent rulers for their expansion campaigns into Wales and Ireland. The depiction itself is taken from the present-day commemorative plaque on the Victoria Monument in Castle Street, which marks its original site.

The 'Three Graces' – namely the Liver Building, Cunard Building and Port of Liverpool Building, which form the centrepiece of Liverpool's classic cityscape identified worldwide – together symbolise the great achievements, commercial success and power enjoyed by the city as a world centre for insurance, shipping and dock construction.

The placement of St George's Hall at the very top of the composition symbolically mirrors the positioning of the building in reality, which – in keeping with Victorian Liverpool's presentation of itself to the rest of the world as the 'new Athens' – sits, like the Parthenon, on a plateau overlooking the city.

In essence, the Hall was built to reflect the Victorian ideals of Truth and Justice (represented by its law courts) and Power and Glory (represented by both its neo-classical architecture and its concert hall) – ideals which are represented by the flowers in the corners of the painting's border: Tiger Lily, symbolising Power because of their 'turkscaps' or turban-shaped flowers (turbans are a symbol of royal status in the East); Peony, symbolising Glory; white Chrysanthemum, symbolising Truth and Rudbeckia, symbolising Justice.

Christopher Columbus's coat of arms represents the explorer's 'discovery' of the Americas and the resulting establishment of the transatlantic trade route, which had a huge impact on the rapid expansion of Liverpool and its rise to become 'the second city of the [British] Empire'. This impact is acknowledged by the scroll text, which is quoted from an inscription on a statue of him outside the Palm House in Sefton Park and reads:

'The Discoverer of America was the making of Liverpool.'

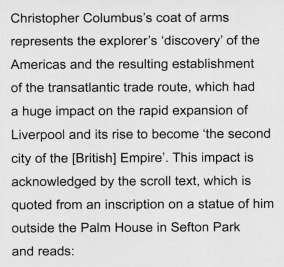

The Empire State Building symbolises Liverpool's rise from 'medieval obscurity to Victorian global pre-eminence' as specifically expressed by the following quote from the Illustrated London News in 1886:

'Liverpool … has become a wonder of the world. It is the New York of Europe, a world city rather than merely British Provincial.'

And the comparison between the two cities is one which has been made by several writers ever since.

City of Achievement

Neptune's iconography, from his attire and the objects he carries to his tattoos, represents Liverpool and the Merseyside area's achievements and innovations throughout history across the fields of science, social welfare and education.

A detail from a stained glass window in the original Liverpool Children's Infirmary, Britain's first children's hospital, which opened in 1851.

The Malaria Knowledge Programme logo, symbolising the discovery of the link between the mosquito and the transmission of malaria by Nobel Laureate Ronald Ross, lecturer at the Liverpool School of Tropical Medicine, in 1902.

The British Rail logo, representing the world's first passenger railway line, built by the Liverpool & Manchester Railway Company. The first train left from Liverpool's Edge Hill, the oldest operational station in the world, which opened in 1830.

The St John's Ambulance logo, symbolising Britain's first purpose-built ambulances introduced by Liverpool in 1886.

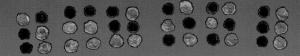

The word 'school' written in Braille, representing Britain's first school for the blind, founded in 1791 by Liverpool-born Edward Rushton.

The emblem of the Boy Scouts. The world's first Boy Scout Troop was founded in Birkenhead in 1908.

The logo of the School of Veterinary Science – Britain's first – established by Liverpool University in 1904.

A detail from the mosaics decorating the perimeter of St George's in Everton – the first all-cast iron church, built in 1814.

The symbol for Physics, representing Liverpool graduate Charles Glover Barkia's winning of the Nobel Prize for Physics 1917.

The Chakra Mandala symbol for Ether, representing the first use of Ether as an anaesthetic in 1776.

The Bowl of Hygeia symbol, representing 'The Dispensary', the world's first chemist, which opened in Liverpool's Princes Street in 1778.

Liverpool-born singer, Lita Roza, the first woman to top the pop charts.

The logo of the Sankey Canal, the UK's first artificial inland waterway built since Roman times and the first canal of the Industrial Revolution.

59

This detail represents the world's first public radio transmission, made from Liverpool's Lewis's department store to the clock tower of the Victoria Building in Liverpool University by Professor Oliver Lodge in 1896.

The graduation gown and mortarboard represent Liverpool as a city of academic excellence.

The logo of the Roy Castle Foundation for Lung Cancer Research, the world's first dedicated cancer research centre.

The logo of the School of Veterinary Science – Britain's first – established by Liverpool University in 1904.

The centre prong of Neptune's trident symbolises the world's first harbour radar tower, which was inaugurated in Liverpool in 1948.

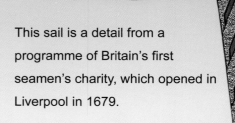

Oh hear us when we cry to thee for those in peril on the sea

This sail is a detail from a programme of Britain's first seamen's charity, which opened in Liverpool in 1679.

The x-ray plate symbolises Britain's first recorded use of x-ray photography for medical diagnosis (by University of Liverpool professor, Oliver Lodge, to locate a bullet in a patient's hand) in 1896.

A lifebelt bearing the RNLI logo represents the first-ever lifeboat service, created at Formby in 1776.

The book acknowledges the significant role that Bidston semaphore station played in Liverpool's maritime economy, guiding ships safely into the port. Also, the first lighthouses in the world to use parabolic mirrors were built at Bidston and Hoylake by Liverpool Dock Master, Captain William Hutchinson, in 1763.

Wedged inside the book is a ticket for Liverpool's Lyceum Library, Europe's first lending library, started in 1757.

A parabolic lighthouse reflecting mirror, developed by Liverpool's first Dock Master, Captain William Hutchinson, in 1763.

Masonic compass and set-square, representing Liverpool's appointment of Britain's first Borough Engineer, James Newlands, in 1847.

A Caduceus, symbolising Britain's first Medical Officer of Health, Dr Duncan, appointed in 1847.

The circle and cross symbol of Venus, which is hooked on top of the Caduceus denotes Britain's first qualified female doctor, who opened her practice in Liverpool in 1884.

A detail from a 1912 booklet created by the Liverpool branch of the RSPCA, the world's oldest animal welfare society, which was started in 1809 as the 'Liverpool Society for Preventing Wanton Cruelty to Brute Animals' to protect animals that worked at the port.

The world's first publicly-funded wash house and baths was opened on Liverpool's Upper Frederick Street in 1842. (The image of the ship is borrowed from an advert for the, privately run, Liverpool floating bath, launched in 1816.)

Britain's first gorilla arrived at Liverpool docks in 1851.

The world's first passenger hovercraft service sailed between Leasowe on the Wirral (symbolised by the gateway to Leasowe Castle) and Rhyl in north Wales in 1962.

MS Agamemnon and USS Niagara laying the first transatlantic telegraph cable, which was manufactured by Liverpool-based RS Newall & Co.

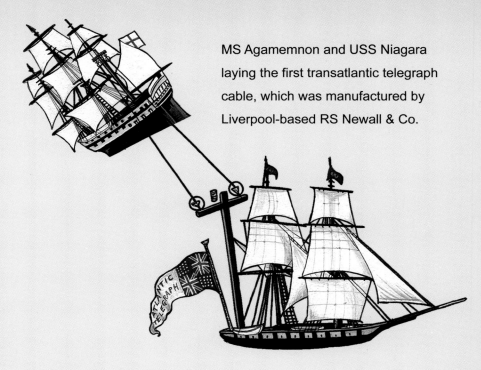

George's Dock building, the ventilation shaft of the Queensway Mersey Railway Tunnel, the world's first underwater rail tunnel.

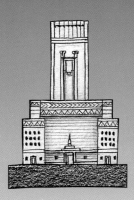

A man riding a Velocipede, representing Britain's first cycling club, 'Liverpool Velocipedes', founded in 1867.

Britannia, the first steamship built by Cunard, which operated the world's first regular transatlantic Royal Mail and fare-paying passenger service from Liverpool to Boston in 1840. The Cunard Steamship Company and Royal Mail Steam Packet Company are symbolised by their House flags, which bear the emblem of the crowned lion holding a globe and of the crown on a red saltire, respectively.

This detail symbolises the Liverpool Overhead Railway (known locally as the 'Docker's Umbrella', which was the world's first electric elevated railway, founded in 1888.

Aerial view of Albert Dock, denoting the great achievement in engineering made by Liverpool in dock construction (the world's first commercial wet dock opened in 1715) and the part this played in the city's rise to the status of a greatly admired world port. The reflection of the Pyramids of Egypt in the dock symbolises such admiration, as expressed by Ramsey Muir, who wrote in his 1907 'History of Liverpool':

'For seven and a quarter miles ... the monumental granite ... front the river in a vast sea wall as solid as the Pyramids, the most stupendous work of its kind that the will and power of man has ever created ....'

The Dock Master's house, Albert Dock, symbolising Liverpool's appointment of the UK's first Dock Master, William Hutchinson, in 1759.

Liverpool Anglican Cathedral, Britain's largest and the world's fifth largest cathedral.

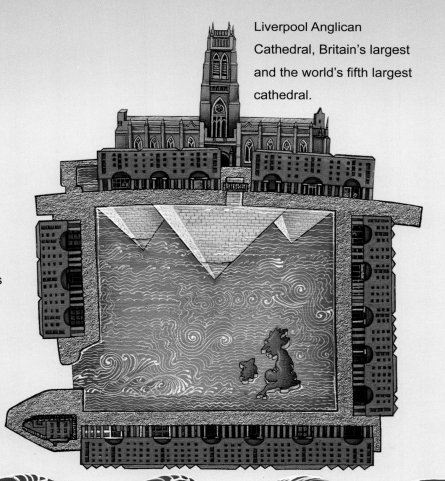

City of Arts, Entertainment...

Triton's staff symbolises Liverpool's strong presence within the film and TV industry – both on a local and international level.

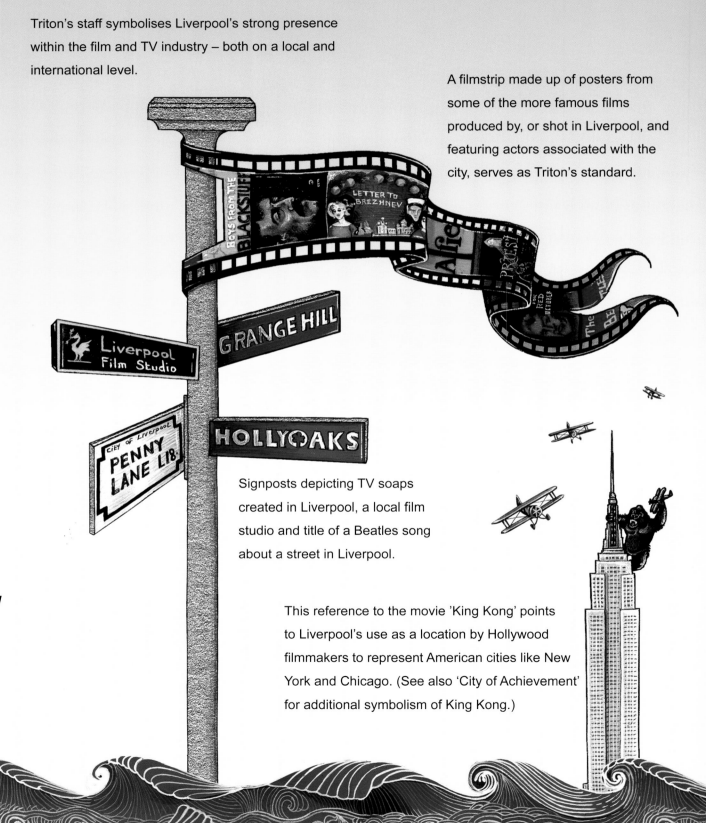

A filmstrip made up of posters from some of the more famous films produced by, or shot in Liverpool, and featuring actors associated with the city, serves as Triton's standard.

Triton's personal iconography – with its maritime associations – has been modified to reflect Liverpool's modern identity as a city of excellence in the fields of the arts, entertainment and sport.

Signposts depicting TV soaps created in Liverpool, a local film studio and title of a Beatles song about a street in Liverpool.

This reference to the movie 'King Kong' points to Liverpool's use as a location by Hollywood filmmakers to represent American cities like New York and Chicago. (See also 'City of Achievement' for additional symbolism of King Kong.)

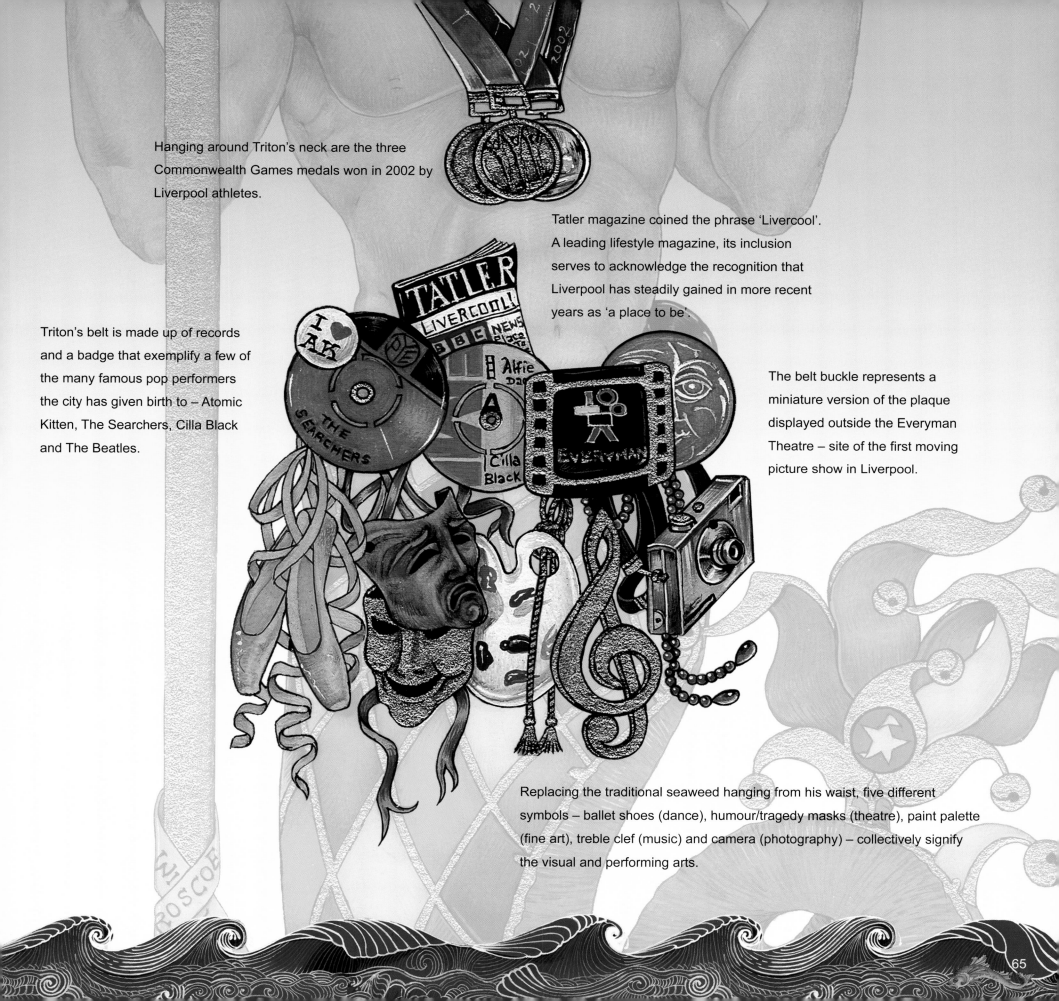

Hanging around Triton's neck are the three Commonwealth Games medals won in 2002 by Liverpool athletes.

Tatler magazine coined the phrase 'Livercool'. A leading lifestyle magazine, its inclusion serves to acknowledge the recognition that Liverpool has steadily gained in more recent years as 'a place to be'.

Triton's belt is made up of records and a badge that exemplify a few of the many famous pop performers the city has given birth to – Atomic Kitten, The Searchers, Cilla Black and The Beatles.

The belt buckle represents a miniature version of the plaque displayed outside the Everyman Theatre – site of the first moving picture show in Liverpool.

Replacing the traditional seaweed hanging from his waist, five different symbols – ballet shoes (dance), humour/tragedy masks (theatre), paint palette (fine art), treble clef (music) and camera (photography) – collectively signify the visual and performing arts.

Triton's traditional crown is replaced with a feathered headdress from Liverpool's Brouhaha carnival.

The fish-scales on Triton's merman tail have been 'dressed' in the style of a court jester's garb to symbolise the theme of entertainment generally but, more specifically, the humour for which Liverpool is renowned and which has produced many famous comedians.

Instead of a conch shell, Triton now holds a microphone, symbolising Liverpool's rich pop music culture.

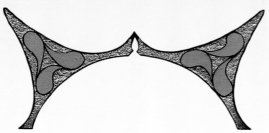

Logos of 'Creamfields'(in blue), a major annual dance music festival held by the people behind Liverpool's famous Cream clubbing brand.

The Liverpool Biennial, the UK's largest international contemporary visual arts festival, is represented by its distinctive coloured checkered logo (serving as the twisted 'wreath' of traditional heraldry on the new Liverpool Coat of Arms.

A decorative motif from the gateway to Mathew Street, which lends its name to one of the biggest international music festivals, held annually in Liverpool.

'Super Lamb Banana', 'Sea Circle' (incorporated into Triton's tail) and 'Spaghetti Horse' – three of Liverpool's well-known public sculptures – represent the city's support for public art.

...and Sport

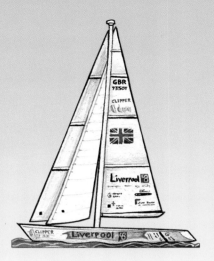

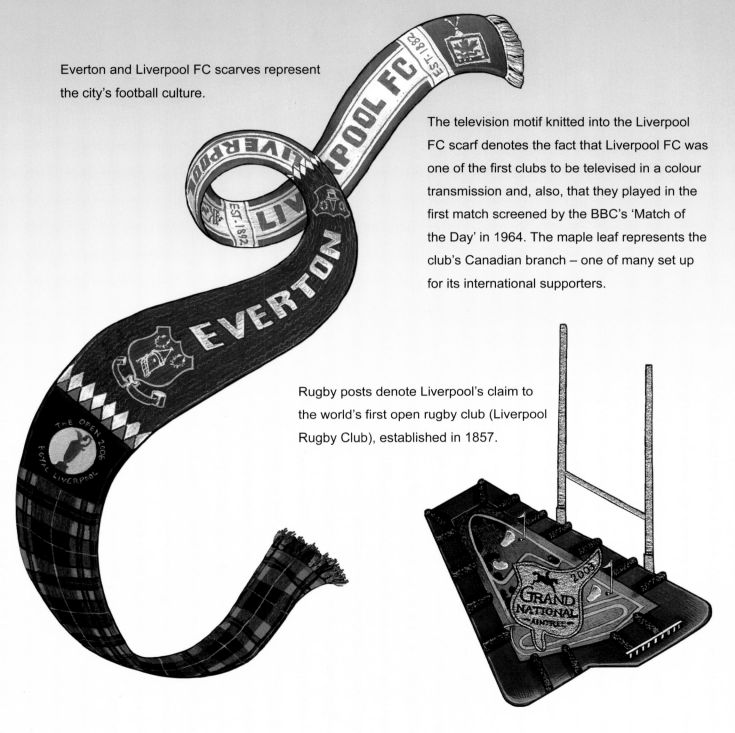

Everton and Liverpool FC scarves represent the city's football culture.

A yacht from the Round the World Yacht Race (for which Liverpool has been the starting and finishing point on several occasions) represents the many international festivals and races that take place on the River Mersey.

The television motif knitted into the Liverpool FC scarf denotes the fact that Liverpool FC was one of the first clubs to be televised in a colour transmission and, also, that they played in the first match screened by the BBC's 'Match of the Day' in 1964. The maple leaf represents the club's Canadian branch – one of many set up for its international supporters.

Rugby posts denote Liverpool's claim to the world's first open rugby club (Liverpool Rugby Club), established in 1857.

Details of Liverpool Aintree racecourse, the Grand National shield, and a 2006 Open Golf tournament scarf represent some of the international sporting events hosted by Liverpool and Merseyside.

City with a Political Conscience

Two of the banners used at the anti-Iraq war demonstration for the visit of the US Secretary of State, Condoleeza Rice, to Liverpool in 2006.

Whilst signifying a city whose past glory was built on the plight of the African people, the anti-slavery token (used by the Abolitionist movement to promote their cause) also symbolises Liverpool's role in opposing the Slave Trade under the leadership of one of its citizens, William Roscoe.

Around the token is Liverpool's Black History Month Group logo. This symbolises the city's acknowledgment of its role in perpetrating the Slave Trade (a formal apology was issued in 1999) as well as the steps that are being taken in modern times to address that part of its history.

The 'Fathers for Justice' protestor who made the news when he chained himself to a 200-ft crane in Liverpool dressed as Batman.

The white and black banner represents the campaign to save Liverpool's iconic warehouse store, Quiggins, which was all but demolished to make way for the development of a new shopping, residential and leisure centre – 'Liverpool ONE' – in the lead-up to the city's year as European Capital of Culture.

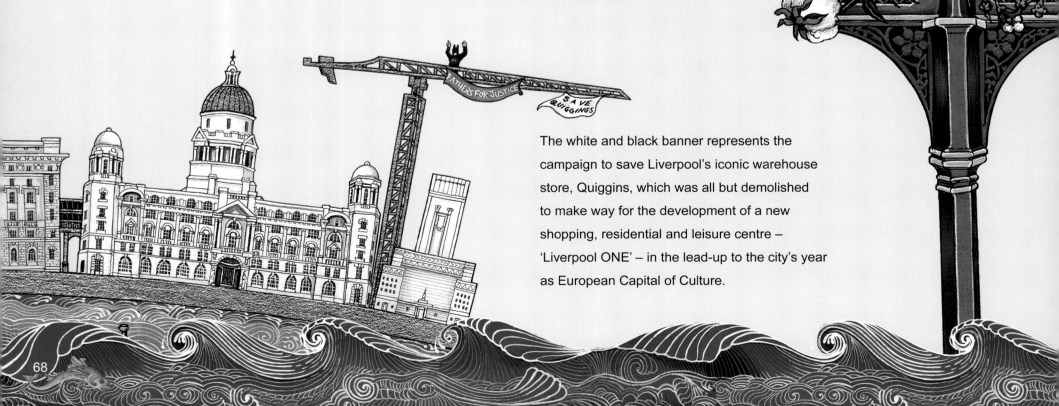

City of Tourism and Leisure

The aeroplane and trail is a detail from the souvenir brochure of the official opening of Speke Airport (now Liverpool John Lennon Airport), one of the oldest operational airports in the UK. Tulip motifs have been added to symbolise Britain's first scheduled flight to Amsterdam, made from here in 1934.

The iron bridge in Sefton Park (Liverpool's most famous park), serves to symbolise the green leisure areas provided by the city.

The entrance to 'The Beatles Story' exhibition, voted the No.1 tourist attraction in the UK.

The tourist bus, symbolising Liverpool's world-class tourist attractions.

These suitcases represent Britain's first package holiday, which flew from Liverpool Airport to France in 1952.

The 'I Love Liverpool' mug, representing Liverpool's fast-growing tourism industry.

'Eight Days a Week', an exchange programme founded in 1998 between Liverpool and Cologne, represents the international profile of Liverpool's arts scene.

City of Cultural Heritage...

The Palm House in Sefton Park represents the city's rich botanical collection, started by William Roscoe in 1799.

Liverpool's original motto: 'DEUS NOBIS HAEC OTIA FECIT' ('God has given us this leisure'), which – in the light of the city's modern image as a city of art and culture – remains as relevant today as when it was first adopted.

The Bluecoat, Liverpool's oldest remaining building (completed 1718) and Britain's first arts centre, founded in 1927.

The coat of arms of William Roscoe (1753–1831), symbolising his role as a leading promoter of cultural development in Liverpool during the late 18th and early 19th centuries. His social and philanthropic activities have earned him the title 'Liverpool's greatest citizen' and 'the founder of Liverpool culture'.

An architectural detail from Britain's first Mosque, which opened on Mount Vernon Street in 1887.

The Walker, Britain's first public art gallery, which opened in 1877, suffered bomb damage in the Second World War.

The Duomo of Florence, symbolising 19th-century Liverpool's craving for recognition as the 'Florence of the North' and, in particular, William Roscoe's dream of making his city a European cultural centre to rival Renaissance Florence – a dream which was fulfilled when Liverpool became 'European Capital of Culture' in 2008.

...and Diversity

The shield represents the most important aspect of Liverpool's identity, its people, who come from many different ethnic backgrounds. This cultural mosaic is symbolised by the 'jigsaw' contained within the shield and the border surrounding it. Each jigsaw piece is decorated with a different pattern, taken from the artistic traditions of the main communities existing in Liverpool – African, Greek, Indian, Persian/Islamic, Chinese, European (German and Italian) and Celtic (Irish). Meanwhile, the missing piece of the jigsaw signifies the further enrichment of Liverpool's multicultural identity by settlers yet to come.

Part of Liverpool folklore and the internationally recognised symbol of Liverpool, the Liverbird at the shield's centre represents the common identity shared by the people of Liverpool – as 'Liverpudlians' – regardless of their ethnic origins.

A projection of a scene from the classic Hindi movie, 'Mughal-E-Azam', from Liverpool's FACT (Foundation for Art and Creative Technology) building represents how culturally diverse communities in Liverpool, as elsewhere, are contributing to and reshaping mainstream British culture.

Pomegranates – the Hebrew/Greco-Roman symbol of multiplicity in unity and rejuvenation – symbolise the culturally diverse and lively character of Liverpool.

Liverpool Playhouse is Britain's oldest repertory theatre company. At its centre is a poster of the musical 'Blood Brothers' (a play set in Liverpool, by Liverpool playwright, lyricist and composer Willy Russell), which is said to be one of the longest-running works of musical theatre in history and points to Liverpool's tradition of inspiring writers and producing successful creative talent.

Liverpool's 'Imperial Arch' (the largest outside China) marks the entrance to Chinatown – the oldest established Chinese community in Europe.

The banner of Milapfest, the UK's all-year-round Indian arts festival, represents the diversity of Liverpool's arts scene. To its left, another banner depicting Guru Nanak, the founder of Sikhism, serves to acknowledge the 500th anniversary of the religion, celebrated in 2007 alongside Liverpool's 800th birthday.

City of Regeneration and Rebirth

The Tower of Liverpool (built in 1405), like the representation of Liverpool Castle, serves as a reminder of the vital role that Liverpool played in English history as a medieval military stronghold. However, being fused with the modern 'Tower Building' that currently stands on its original site, it also symbolises, simultaneously, both the celebration of the regeneration of the city and the mourning of the loss of some of its most historically important structures.

As a symbol of regeneration, the eight-pointed star above St George's Hall denotes the renovation and reopening of the building in 2007 – a major event in the city's 800th anniversary celebrations.

The construction crane symbolises the continuing development of the Liverpool cityscape and also the regeneration of the city in the lead-up to 2008, the year it celebrated its status as European Capital of Culture.

The Radisson hotel tower block and FACT buildings together symbolise the regeneration of modern Liverpool.

As the symbol of arts and learning in Hindu mythology, the swan denotes Liverpool's new identity as European Capital of Culture.

The wings of a Red Admiral butterfly form a half-flower motif which mimics that seen in Liverpool's original coat of arms. The name of the butterfly alludes to Liverpool's past maritime identity, whilst the butterfly motif itself, as a symbol of metamorphosis, also denotes the transformation of that identity. Therefore, the placement of the butterfly motif between the Liverbird and Swan is significant because, collectively, this imagery can be interpreted (from the bottom symbol up) as: Liverpool's old identity (Liverbird) is reborn (butterfly) into its new identity (swan).

The piece of seaweed, traditionally held in the beak of the Liverbird as a symbol of Liverpool's maritime/mercantile identity, has been replaced by a pen and paintbrush to signify the city's move towards a new identity as a city of arts and culture.

A spider, symbol of fate/destiny, connects the two halves of the painting's composition – ie the Past and the Present – with its web, symbolising the importance of Liverpool looking to the future whilst continuing to value its rich heritage. The spider's act of spinning its web also serves as a visual analogy for the creation of Liverpool's story (as in the phrase 'spin a tale').

Angela Heslop

I am a producer at BBC Radio Merseyside, and have been involved with radio for many years. It really is the most exciting and powerful medium to work in. I have always been passionate about the arts, and have been very privileged, working in radio, to be able to express and reflect that passion. I always say the pictures are better on the radio.

My work in BBC local Radio takes me into the heart of communities and one of the main highlights was co-ordinating and producing BBC Radio Merseyside's coverage of Liverpool's Year of European Capital of Culture in 2008. It was an exciting year and being able to reflect the diverse culture of those twelve months, put new voices on the radio and bring many of the events 'live' to our listeners was particularly special.

It has been a great pleasure to work with Amrit and Rabindra over the years. Their work is so stimulating, beautiful, moving, and skilled. Their exquisite paintings always tell a story, and it has been a privilege to report on their artistic talent and commitment to the arts in general.

An Interview
with Angela Heslop

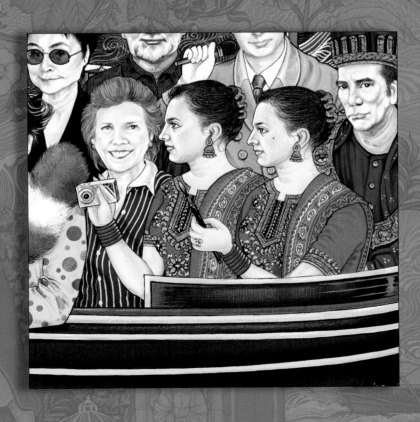

The Making of Liverpool Animation

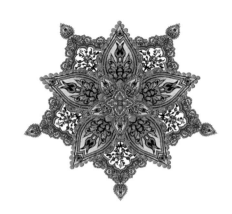

Angela Heslop:

Amrit and Rabindra, what was the inspiration for 'The Making of Liverpool'?

Well, the animation was based on our public painting commission 'Liverpool 800'. So that was the initial inspiration for the film in terms of its visual content and storyline. But there were several reasons for making it. In the first instance the idea was sparked by popular public demand to know more about the painting and the specific details of what it was portraying about Liverpool.

Initially we intended just to write a text commentary for display alongside the original artwork. But we have always wanted to explore our creative potential through digital technology and the medium of moving imagery, so decided instead to test the waters and tell the story of the painting through animation.

At the same time we wanted to look beyond the painting itself and make a film that gave some insight into our artistic connection with Liverpool, as well as our working relationship and practice as painters.

Right. 'The Making of Liverpool' animation, official poster.
Above. The Singh Twins with 'Liverpool 800' at Liverpool St George's Hall.

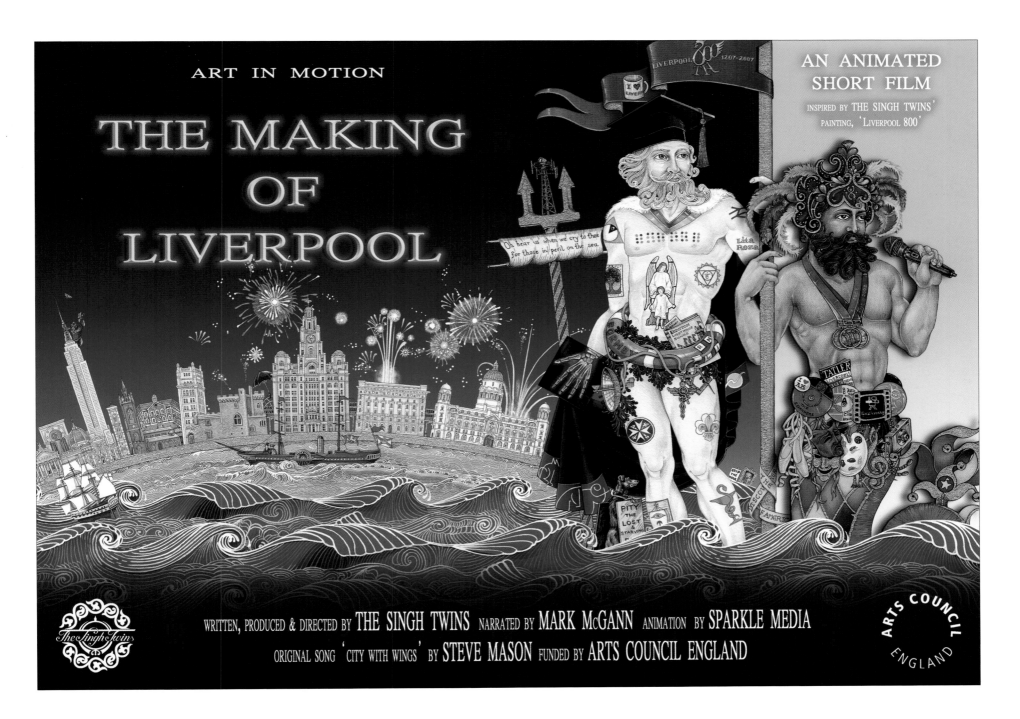

Finally, it was made as an expression of the personal pride we have for our home city, which extended to our wanting to showcase the creative talent of our local area generally and how Liverpool itself continues to inspire creativity across the arts. In this respect, we were very clear from the outset that the animation should have a collaborative element, featuring ourselves as the visual artists but also involving animators, musicians and performance artists with a Liverpool connection. We were very fortunate to find a great team for the project comprising Andy Cooper and his fellow animators at Sparkle Media, singer songwriter Steve Mason and actor Mark McGann.

Angela Heslop:

Had you used animation before in your work?

No. Never.

Angela Heslop:

But film you have?

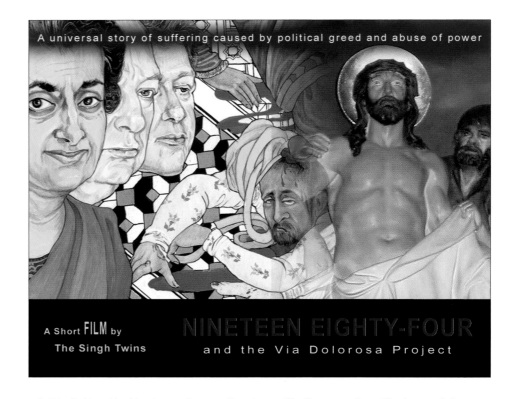

A universal story of suffering caused by political greed and abuse of power

A Short FILM by
The Singh Twins

NINETEEN EIGHTY-FOUR
and the Via Dolorosa Project

Yes. As far back as we can remember we have had a fascination for film. In fact, if we hadn't been artists we would have been filmmakers. But when we were going through the education system the opportunities just didn't seem to be there, so we never considered filmmaking a viable career option. However, in between university degrees, we had some time on our hands and took the opportunity to enrol on a local college course where we gained some training in video production.

Several years later we made our first film – a short documentary about one of our other paintings titled 'Nineteen Eighty-Four', which depicts the Indian Government's military attack on the Golden Temple at Amritsar, one of the most historic and sacred shrines of the Sikhs, in 1984. The film focuses on the human tragedy of the event and the related pogroms against the Sikhs which took place later that year, highlighting the universal nature of innocent suffering caused by political corruption and greed, and making the Sikh experience of 84 more relevant to wider audiences through a comparison with the Via Dolorosa tradition

of Christianity that explores the humiliation and suffering of Jesus in the final hours leading to his crucifixion.

Although technology had progressed tremendously with everything going digital by then, we knew enough basics to produce the whole project on our own. But it's a straightforward narration approach using video footage, archival newspaper imagery, photo material and digitally simulated pans of the painting. No animation.

Right. 'Nineteen Eighty-Four'. The Singh Twins, 1999.
Above. 'Nineteen Eighty-Four and the Via Dolorosa Project ', official film poster.

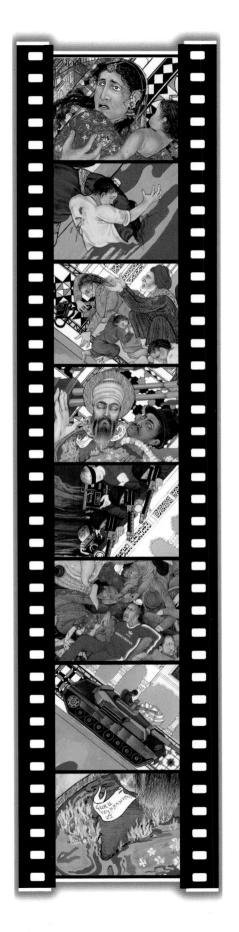

Angela Heslop:

So how did you create 'The Making of Liverpool'? Perhaps you could talk to us a little about the process.

Starting with the 'Liverpool 800' painting, the first thing we had to do was decide on a story or logical narrative for the animation to follow. So we sat down and composed a poem that chronologically picked out the main features of Liverpool's history as represented through the various details in that work. This provided the main narration for the film and a basis for the storyboard we created for Sparkle Media, which gave line-by-line directions as to how we wanted the poem to translate visually. From the storyboard the animators put together an animatic or rough edit of the basic animation sequences. Setting simulating camera movement across various parts of the painting to an audio recording of the poem to show how the various actions and transition we had described to them would happen on screen. This gave us an overview of the kind of direction the final animation would take.

Once the storyboard was finalised we discovered that there is a lot of preparation to be done before the actual task of animation can begin. One of the first things we had to do was take a digital copy of the 'Liverpool 800' painting apart. Luckily we had scanned the painting at different stages of its development and already had very high-quality image files of both the completed artwork and close-up details from it to work with.

For our part, we didn't have a hands-on knowledge of actual animation software, but we did have a lot of experience in manipulating still imagery, so we helped the animation team with the groundwork, separating every different visual element within the painting to create main characters and objects to use in the animation. Each of those then had to be digitally dissected into their smaller parts and components, which were then individually named and saved as a new file image, or on different layers of a single file image which could be manipulated independently of the main character if need be. Of course, each time we cut anything out from the painting or main characters and objects it produced a hole, which then had to be digitally cloned back in or repainted to repair the damage and ensure that all the objects, characters and their backgrounds appeared complete again, in themselves, when used in the animation.

Right. Sequential documentation of details from the 'Liverpool 800' painting.

Above and right. Different pre-animation preparation stages – separating characters and objects from the original painted artwork, repairing the background, creating missing details such as the corner of the oil rig, and replacing the cut-outs to their original position, ready for animation.

Left. One of The Singh Twins' other paintings titled 'Partners in Crime: Deceptions and Lies', which was used in a sequence of 'The Making of Liverpool'.

There were some instances where we couldn't just extract and use imagery exactly as it appeared in the painting. For example, one of the characters in the artwork carries a flag in the form of a filmstrip depicting scenes from the movies. This was painted curved and wavy as though blowing in the wind. But this was useless to the animation team as it wasn't something they could manipulate effectively with their software. What they needed was a much more structured and organised image. So we had to first digitally recreate the flag, using various drawing and colour-fill tools to make it looked stretched out and flat. Into this we cut and pasted all the little movie poster images from the original painting and, using stretch, skew and clone tools, reshaped those to fit the new flattened version of the flag.

It was a very time-consuming process but the animators then had something they could import directly into their animation software to create the movement effects they wanted, such as gravity force to make the flag go up and down and a wind generator to simulate waving motion.

Left. A detail of the flag from the original 'Liverpool 800' painting.
Inset Left. Initial drawing of the flag and a still from the animated film sequence in which it was used.
Right. The digitally reconstructed, flattened flag, *front and reverse side*.

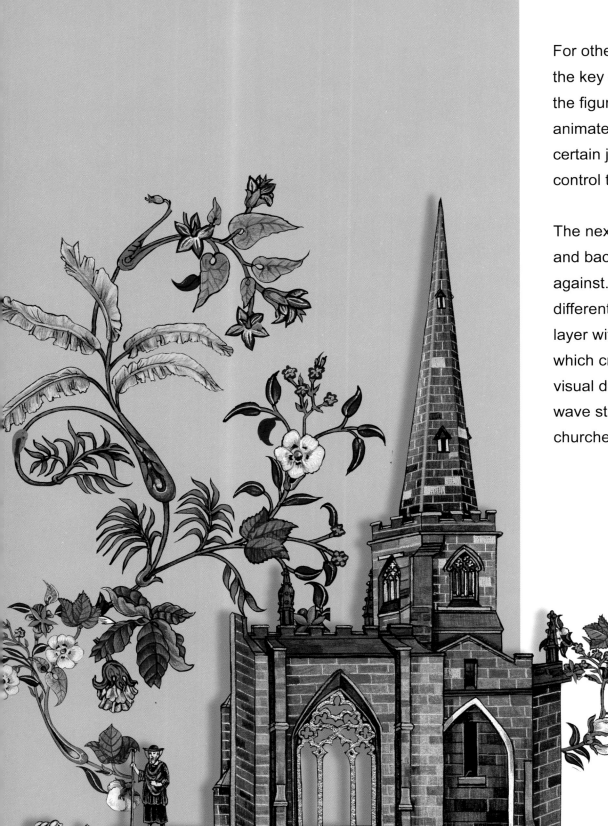

For other parts of the film where we wanted to animate some of the key characters, as for example with the rowing monks scene, the figures were first dissected into their various parts, then animated using a puppet tool which allowed the animators to fix certain joints or pivot points around which to create actions and control the direction of movement.

The next thing the animators had to do was create the scenery and backdrops for the characters and key objects to move against. The more complicated ones involved assembling different elements from the painting on their own transparent layer within the same scene and applying drop shadows to each, which created a sense of distance between them and added visual depth. Looking at the rowing monks scene again, each sea wave strip had its own layer, as did the monks in their boat, the churches, the clouds and the sky.

One of the final stages in the making process was the application of special effects to create atmosphere – such as the lightning, the rain and creative lighting around the edge of the frame.

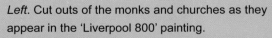

Left. Cut outs of the monks and churches as they appear in the 'Liverpool 800' painting.

Above top to bottom. Puppet characters of the monks created for the animation, indicating the location of some of the pivot points or joints around which motion was created.

Right top and middle. Two stills from the monks' scene in 'The Making of Liverpool' showing lighting and rain effects.

Right bottom. Cut outs of other elements used for different animated layers of the sequence.

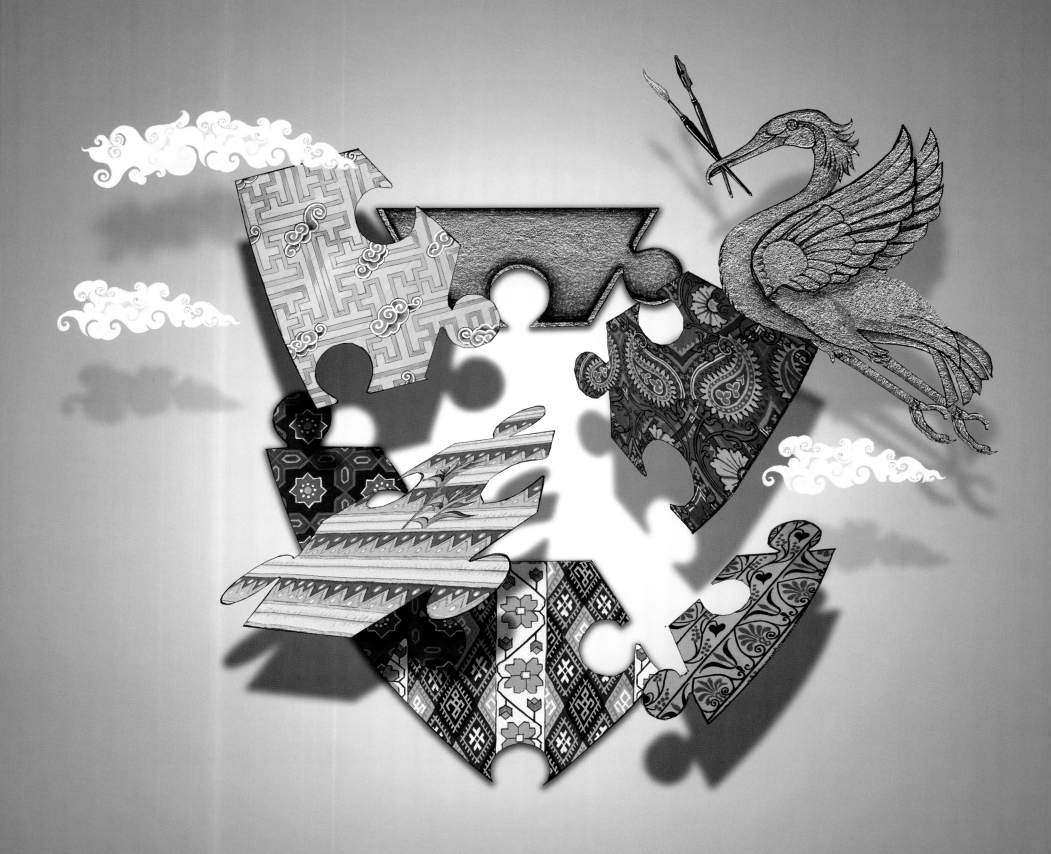

In a couple of places the animators used 3D animation. For example, there is a sequence in which different pieces of a jigsaw puzzle fly into screen and reassemble in the shape of the Liverpool coat of arms, or shield. In addition to shadow and lighting effects this required the use of other processes, such as simulated camera angles, skewing and rotation action, which was applied to each piece of the puzzle on its own time line or motion path to create the illusion of their moving independently but interrelated through 3D space.

Far left. 3D simulation of the 'Liverpool 800' coat of arms animated jigsaw sequence.
Left. The coat of arms shield as it appears in the 'Liverpool 800' painting.
Above. Two stills from the coat of arms 3D jigsaw puzzle sequence.

One of our favourite sequences in the animation is the one which brings our image of Neptune, one of the key characters in the film, to life, step by step. In terms of other technical processes that were used in the animation, this is where our usual practice as artists to document our work proved to be very useful, because we had already digitally scanned every stage and detail of its production from the original drawing to the completed work. So, for part of this sequence the animators were able to overlay the different stages we had documented for Neptune and have them play chronologically in rapid succession to magical effect.

Far left. Detail of Neptune from the 'Liverpool 800' painting.
Left. The original drawing of Neptune.
Above. Two stills from the 'painting in' Neptune sequence of the animation.

Here and overleaf. Digitally scanned stages in the painting process for Neptune, used in the animation.

For the final part of 'The Making of Liverpool' animation we wanted to give audiences a glimpse of the real city. So we decided to integrate animated elements from our painting with photographic imagery of Liverpool. One of the sequences in this section of the film uses a photo of the city's classic waterfront, which required some preparation work before it could be incorporated in to the film. To begin with we took different photographs of the city along the same horizontal line of vision, looking across the River Mersey to Liverpool. We then imported these into the computer, placing them side-by-side on the same page and, using basic cloning techniques, removed the joins to create a single panoramic view of the cityscape for the animators to input into the film and overlay with animated details from our painting.

As with all the techniques employed in the making of the animation it was a very time-consuming process.

Angela Heslop:

I was going to say time-consuming because the detail in the animation is meticulous. And I just wondered how long it took to achieve the film?

It took the best part of six months, once all the preparation work had been done, to put the actual animation together.

Right. Stills from 'The Making of Liverpool' showing the integration of photographic elements with animated artwork.

Angela Heslop:

The first time I saw the film, the colours really struck me because they are so vibrant and beautiful. Is colour important in your work?

Colour is very important, yes. And we think that's something we have generally inherited from our Indian background where colour is just part of everyday life – from the clothes we wear to the food we eat. But vivid, contrasting colour is also characteristic of the Indian miniature tradition of painting that has most influenced our own art. That in itself is reflected in the animation, because one thing we were certain about from the outset was that the painting which inspired the film should not be entirely lost through the process of animation because we wanted the animation overall to maintain both the painterly quality and aesthetic style we are known for. In addition, we have always been interested in the symbolic meaning and significance of colour and its association, for example with the seasons and human emotion. Again, within Indian culture bright colours are considered auspicious and associated with celebratory occasions. With 'The Making of Liverpool' being a celebration of a city's history and achievements, it was appropriate we felt to maintain that colour palette as far as possible throughout the film.

Right. Images of India showing the importance of colour in Indian culture.
Far right top. 'Summer', 'Autumn', 'Winter' and 'Spring'. The Singh Twins, 2004.
Far right bottom. 'Colours of Life'. The Singh Twins, 2005.

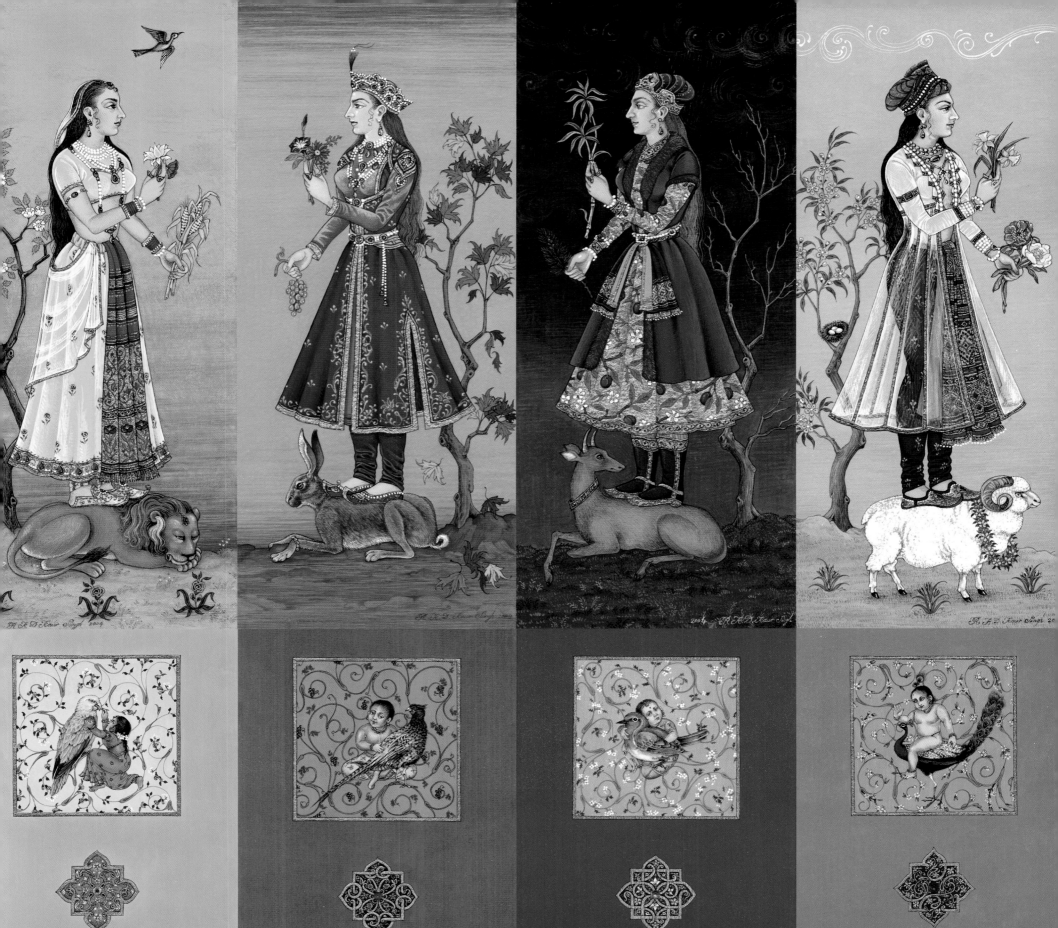

The Singh Twins working on 'Arts Matters'.

Angela Heslop:

What were the main challenges in actually taking part in the process and creating the film?

The first one, which we think every creative person faces, was the challenge of finding funding. But we were very fortunate to get generous support from Arts Council England towards the main production costs.

On a personal level, whilst we ourselves have always worked together and are very in tune with one another creatively, the fact that this was our first collaboration with other artists was a particular challenge in itself. Partly because we were not entirely sure that we could accurately convey, and have translated into a new medium, exactly what we wanted in our own minds, and partly because we were anxious not to stifle the animators' individual creative freedom and push what we wanted at the expense of losing any original ideas the animators might bring to the table.

In the end, we think the collaboration worked extremely well. Sparkle Media were really great to work with and did a brilliant job, we feel, of capturing the vision we had for the animation.

In terms of technical challenges, some of the details depicted in the 'Liverpool 800' painting were just too small to be used because, when enlarged or zoomed into at full screen, they lost definition. There were also a couple of lines in the storyboard for which we didn't initially have any visuals, because they related to things that were only indirectly referenced in the painting.

We got round these problems by sourcing relevant imagery from other paintings we have produced over the years, like 'Dogwood and Yew', 'Two to Tango', 'Manhattan Mall' and 'Steppin' Out with My Baby'.

Right. Sparkle Media showing The Singh Twins some of their initial work on the animation.

Other Paintings Used in 'The Making of Liverpool' Animation.

Left. Thumbnails of other Liverpool-themed paintings used in part for the animation.
Above. A composite of some of the details extracted from other paintings used in the animation.
Right. 'Dogwood and Yew'. The Singh Twins, 2005. (The painting from which the fish were sourced for the animation.)

The original figure of the The Singh Twins is cut out from the 'Liverpool 800' painting (left), and the head removed.

The body is placed as a separate layer on a new background.

Right. 'Two to Tango'. The Singh Twins, 2006. (The Singh Twins' portraits in the 'Liverpool 800' painting, far left, were too small to use large screen in the animation. So for the close-up shots, the heads were replaced with those from this larger scale painting).

And the head replaced with one cut from the
larger painting, 'Two to Tango.'

Left. 'Manhattan Mall'. The Singh Twins, 1997.
Right. 'Steppin' Out with My Baby' ('The Art of Loving' Series). The Singh Twins, 2003.
Below. Details from these two paintings, which appear in the animation.

In some instances we had to create new imagery especially for the animation, such as the letters which fly into the sky across the sea to the Statue of Liberty in a sequence which depicts the first ship to carry passengers and mail across the Atlantic.

Sound was probably one of the bigger challenges for us, as we hadn't had much experience in recording and creating sound for film. There were several aspects to this. One was actually creating the underlying music track to the main narration, which we put together on our laptop using selections of sample music and instrumental effects provided by software that we already had on our system. We also composed some music from scratch using the piano keyboard feature in our software.

Another was creating the ambient sound effects, such as seagulls, aeroplane engines and ships' horns to overlay on the main track, which both we and Sparkle Media sourced again from the pre-existing sound effects within our filmmaking software and purchased from the internet. Then there was the challenge of editing these together smoothly and achieving the correct balance in sound levels between the different audio tracks of music, narration and sound effects.

As creative director for Sparkle Media's team of animators on our project, Andy Cooper had the arduous task of then making sure that everything remained in sync throughout the duration of the film when the various animation sequences they had produced were put together with the final audio tracks.

Manhattan
New York
USA

Above. A still from 'The Making of Liverpool'.

Left. One of the envelopes digitally created for the animation.

For the soundtrack of the final sequence in the animation, we wanted to create a new piece of music that directly responded to the 'Liverpool 800' painting and originally intended to use a song called 'Liverpool Take a Bow', which we had written ourselves and recorded with the help of talented local musicians from the Wirral Musicians Project.

However, during production of the animation we came across Steve Mason's song 'City with Wings' and decided to go with that instead. Mainly because it so perfectly reflected the musical style we were looking for and matched the sentiments and narrative of both our painting and the animation, but also because Steve's involvement opened up another way to develop our collaborative aspirations for the project.

Above. Steve Mason recording 'City with Wings'.
Left. A detail of Triton from the 'Liverpool 800' painting.

Angela Heslop:

Turning now to other collaborators on the project, the narrator for the animation was Mark McGann. Why did you choose him?

As we mentioned earlier, whilst the animation was essentially about bringing our 'Liverpool 800' painting and its story of Liverpool to wider audiences, we also wanted it to profile the creative talent of Liverpool, Merseyside and all the Northwest region. Having a professional narrator for the script enabled us to involve the performance arts. But we wanted to find someone who could bring something extra – with the ability not only to inject emotion, feeling and atmosphere, but whose sense of rhythm and timing would preserve the lyrical character or poetic format of the script. Sparkle Media suggested that one of the McGann brothers, who are a very accomplished and well-known family of actors with strong Liverpool connections, would be an ideal choice. So we contacted them through their official fan website, sending them an outline of the project and copy of the poem not knowing if they would even see our email or have the slightest interest in, or time to be involved in, the project. To our delight, Mark replied immediately saying that he would be thrilled to contribute.

What we particularly liked about Mark, and all the creators on the team, was their genuine enthusiasm for the project. Which was wonderful, because we felt it was essential for the success of the project that the people involved shared our passion for the animation and the city it represented. And we were not disappointed, because everyone took a personal interest in the animation, giving it 100%, and we feel this really shines through in the quality of the final work.

Aside from the film, the friendships we formed through the collaboration were, for us, one of the most valuable and positive things to come out of the experience.

Above left. Mark McGann in some of his many acting roles and on stage.
Above centre. Mark recording the narration for 'The Making of Liverpool'.

111

'City with Wings'

A song by Steve Mason

Standing on the corner, lookin' out across the water

Underneath the shelter of wings

Behind me busy city life, that only stops for traffic lights

Forever changing red, amber and green

Bustling trains below my feet, cars and buses fill the street

Everybody must be runnin' late

Coz only strangers take the time to gaze upon the 'Pool's' design

Albert's in the dock and looking great

This is Home to the seagull, Home to the people

Who smile away their pain and all their fears

This is Home to the laughter, the music ever after

Home to every ship the Mersey brings, yeh

Love red or blue, it's all here for you

In this beautiful city with wings

Now the ghosts of every working man

Who worked here in this shipyard land

Could tell you stories only they could tell

They suffered for the price of coal, to warm the cockles of their souls

And save their families from the freezing hell

But now the future looks so good, the working man gets what he should

Pride's replaced the dignity he lost

Now Merseyside is full of pride, its beauty cannot be denied

Lest we forget the precious lives it cost

This is Home to the people, Home to the seagulls

Who spread their wings and cry 'can you see me'

Home to the laughter, the music ever after

Home to every mariner it brings, yeh

Love red or blue, it's all here for you

In this beautiful city with wings

And from the side of evergreen, two religions can be seen

Praisin' up to the sky

Past and present, future too, merging into something new

Just to take you and I, so high

This is Home to the people, the beautiful people

Home to every traveller it brings, yeh

Love red or blue, it's all here for you

In this beautiful city with wings

See how we fly, in the city with wings

See how we fly, in the city with wings .... Repeat to fade

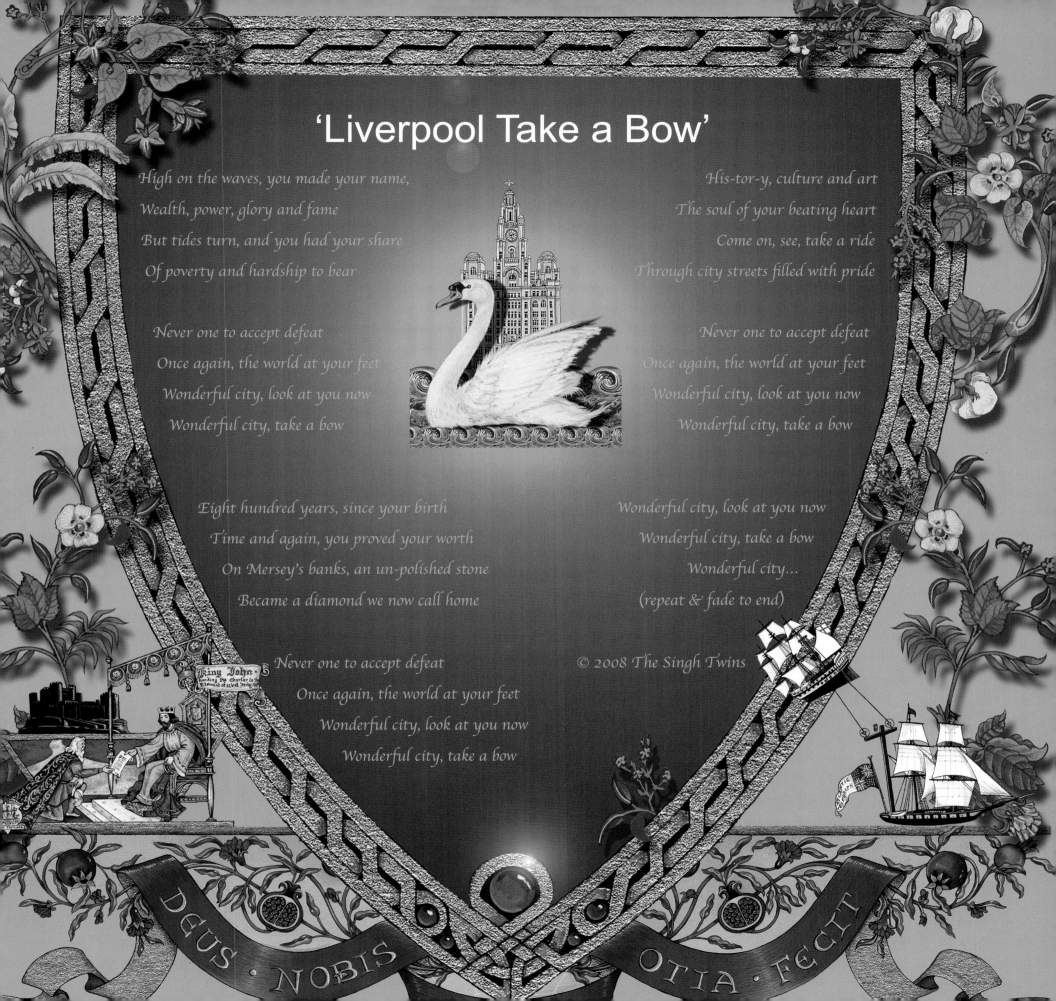

'Liverpool Take a Bow'

High on the waves, you made your name,

Wealth, power, glory and fame

But tides turn, and you had your share

Of poverty and hardship to bear

Never one to accept defeat

Once again, the world at your feet

Wonderful city, look at you now

Wonderful city, take a bow

Eight hundred years, since your birth

Time and again, you proved your worth

On Mersey's banks, an un-polished stone

Became a diamond we now call home

Never one to accept defeat

Once again, the world at your feet

Wonderful city, look at you now

Wonderful city, take a bow

His-tor-y, culture and art

The soul of your beating heart

Come on, see, take a ride

Through city streets filled with pride

Never one to accept defeat

Once again, the world at your feet

Wonderful city, look at you now

Wonderful city, take a bow

Wonderful city, look at you now

Wonderful city, take a bow

Wonderful city…

(repeat & fade to end)

© 2008 The Singh Twins

DEUS · NOBIS · OTIA · FECIT

'The Making of Liverpool'
Animation Narration

From the mouth of a river you came to be
A city of great antiquity.
The Romans arrived many centuries before
The Saxons and Vikings reached your shore.
All left their mark upon your soil
Which Medieval man would learn to toil
Deciding there to populate
To fish and farm and cultivate.
From across the Mersey soon came others
Ferried by the Christian brothers.
All braving the currents till land was made
You quickly became a centre of trade.

Liverpool it's clear to see
How steeped you are in history
From Pool to village to market town
Traders and craftsmen settled down.

Oh hear us when we cry to thee
for those in peril on the sea.

SS PATROCLUS

In 1207 you were granted power
Fortified with castle and tower
With a military fleet in a strategic location
From which to serve the English Nation.
A stronghold that suited a Tudor Queen's plans
To subjugate the Irish clans
Whose deerskin, yarn, sheep and cattle
Continued to flow through times of battle.
Whilst cotton and coal left Liverpool's harbours
Along with the early Pilgrim Fathers
Who crossed the Pond to the USA
There to colonise and to pray.

Liverpool you soon would be
A city whose economy
Would grow to be the very best
Trading globally East and West.

In Victorian times your passenger liner
Across the Atlantic could not be finer.
Other companies would find it hard
To rival the ships of Mr Cunard.
The first in Great Britain to set up sail
In order to carry the Royal Mail
To American cousins across the sea
Living in the land of Liberty.
In an age of industrial revolution
You would often find the solution.
With your steel, two ships were able
To lay the first Atlantic cable.

Liverpool your Victorian might
Built on the African people's plight
For many centuries ruled the waves
In the triangle that traded slaves.

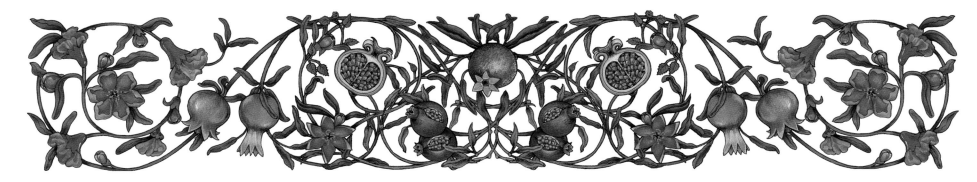

Till one of your own sons saw the light
And determined then to set things right
By leading the movement in the cause
To abolish unjust slavery laws.
Working to set the city apart
As a world-class centre of culture and art
Roscoe dreamt of making his home
A city to rival Florence and Rome.
No doubt he would be pleased to see
The impact of his legacy
A city of creative industry
And tradition of political activity.

Liverpool your cityscape view
Is seen by thousands, forgotten by few
Including citizens marching strong
Against laws and leaders in the wrong.

Your docks were hailed a feat of engineering
To rival the tomb of the Pharaoh king
With solid walls and sturdy quays
A haven from the treacherous seas.
Your Anglican tower caressed by cloud
Is a wonder of architecture, tall and proud
Carved by the masons' skill-full hand
The largest Cathedral in the land.
And with your docks defied all laws
When surviving the Blitz and two world wars.
While other buildings that marked you great
Suffered a much less happy fate.

Liverpool your tale is almost spun
Though your story has just begun
With present and future yet to be told
But still connected to days of old.

Your people from backgrounds rich and poor
Together create such a colourful jigsaw
Of heritage and faiths from across the sea
Producing your unique diversity.
Each have worked hard to earn their place
Carving their image on Liverpool's face
Your new Coat of arms proclaims their part
It puts the people at Liverpool's heart.
Your Liver birds stay, except for one
Transformed now as a graceful swan.
India's symbol of arts and learning
Two paths to which, the city's been turning.

Liverpool your identity
Rooted in trade upon the sea
Is now a shadow of its past
A maritime glory that couldn't last.

Established as a city of academic fame
Whose sons and daughters honoured your name
Through science, invention and innovation
Nobel winners who served the Nation.
And selfless souls who met the needs
Of man and beast through charitable deeds
Leading the way in basic health care
Social works and animal welfare.
Now you're famed for your heritage sites
Offering visitors many delights
Serving their interests and giving pleasure
As a city of tourism and of leisure.

Liverpool home of the Fabulous Four
In truth you offer so much more
With your galleries, parks and city tours
Theatres, museums and shops galore.

Your airport opened in thirty-three
Carrying passengers across the sea
With the first chartered flight to Amsterdam
A doorway to Europe was your plan.
Now, like a butterfly, you are reborn
Awakening to another dawn
Of Hollywood film and TV making
Directors, producers their own forsaking
For Liverpool writers, sets and plots
And buildings that offer those ideal shots.
For those who want to mimic New York
Liverpool's streets are all the talk.

Liverpool, your talent is at the top
Particularly when it comes to pop.
In entertainment you certainly rule
No wonder they call you Livercool.

With singers and songs that break the charts
And a strong tradition in performance arts
Like dance and theatre old and new
Comedy, painting, photography too.
So many names are yours to claim
In Great Britain's Hall of Fame.
Even in the world of sport
Your reputation's far from nought.
City of the reds and blues
And tournaments, which hit the news
Your racing grounds for horse and hound
Are throughout the world, renowned.

Liverpool we paint with pride
Your story so that, far and wide
All will know you've come to be
Europe's Capital, culturally
800 years displayed for all,
beyond the steps of St George's Hall.

Angela Heslop:

How much of the
animation is a
personal view
of the city?

Well, as we mentioned earlier, the animation was intended to
be partly autobiographic documenting not only our ongoing
connection and creative relationship with Liverpool, but offering
an insight into our working processes and interests as artists.
So there are some personal anecdotes and messages in there,
some more obvious than others.

For example, in the final 'City with Wings' song sequence there
is a photographic image of a banner from an art exhibition
entitled 'Sikhs in Print', which we curated as an independent
artist initiative for Milapfest, contributing to Liverpool's wider
celebrations of its official status as European Capital of Culture in
2008. The banner is dominated by the face of an important figure
from Sikh history, Maharaja Duleep Singh, selected from our
private archive of illustrated prints, engravings and memorabilia.
Which is significant in itself, representing not only our academic
background and ongoing interest in Sikh history and art in
general, but also our particular fascination with Maharaja Duleep
Singh and his times.

THE MAHARAJAH OF PATIALA

Near right, above and below. Two artifacts from The Singh Twins' Twin Studio Archive.
Right. The 'Sikhs in Print' exhibition banner.
Far right, top to bottom. A still from 'The Making of Liverpool' animation showing how
the banner was used. Three exhibits from the 'Sikhs in Print' exhibition.
The Singh Twins giving former President of India, Dr Kalam, a private tour of the show.

Details of the Bush-Blair painting, 'Partners in Crime: Deception and Lies'.

There are a couple of references to our personal views on war, such as the animated sequence of an image of Bush and Blair – which in fact is a copy of a painting we produced in 2004 as a response to the Iraq war – and the later sequence about Liverpool's Roman Catholic cathedral and its connection with World Wars I and II, in which a much smaller version of the Bush-Blair image appears alongside a Stop the War placard. These sequences symbolise the time we demonstrated against the then US Secretary of State, Condoleezza Rice's official visit to Liverpool in 2006, carrying placards of both images on a public march. At the same time, the integration of other paintings within the animation were designed to give audiences a wider insight into our work.

In another sequence a portrait of the Indian screen goddess Madhubala is projected from the window of Liverpool's FACT building. She is our favourite Bollywood actress, depicted in full costume in a publicity still from 'Mughal-e-Azam'. Which is an historical epic set in a period of Indian history for which we have a particular fascination and which gave rise to the Imperial style of miniature painting that has had the most significant impact on our art.

Above and centre. 1940s calendar images of Bollywood actress Madhubala and The Singh Twins' painted version, *bottom right*.

Other parts of the animation incorporate visual details such as the 'Eight Days a Week' ribbon and 'Past Modern' exhibition banners. These point not only to the times we have represented Liverpool on an international platform, but how the city has supported and recognised our work over the years. 'Eight Days a Week' was a Liverpool-Cologne artists' exchange project we took part in through the Bluecoat (which, incidentally, also gave us our very first gallery show – a significant turning point in our career). 'Past Modern' was a major retrospective of our work hosted by the Walker Art Gallery.

Left. A photo of The Singh Twins' Walker Art Gallery exhibition banner and a detail of how it is represented in the animation, *below*.

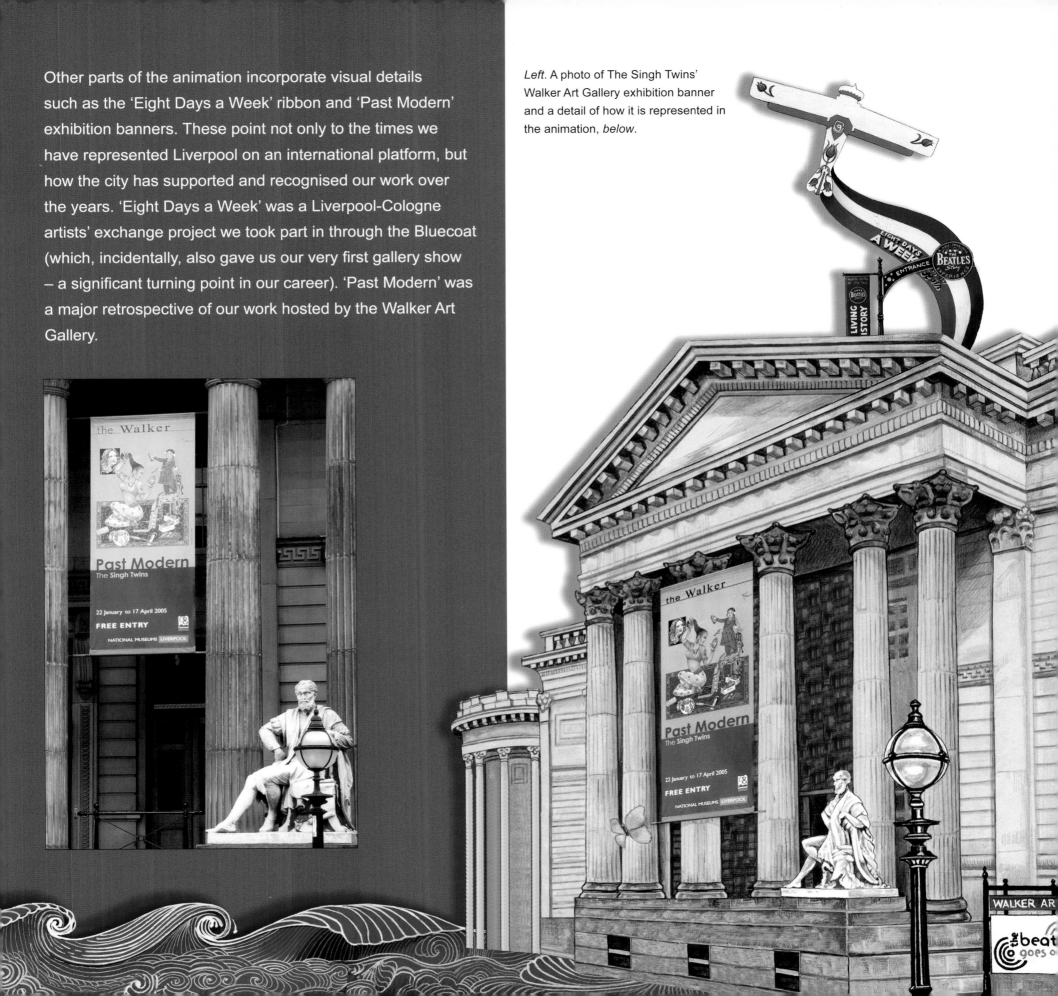

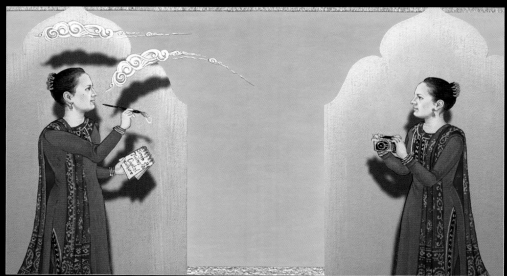

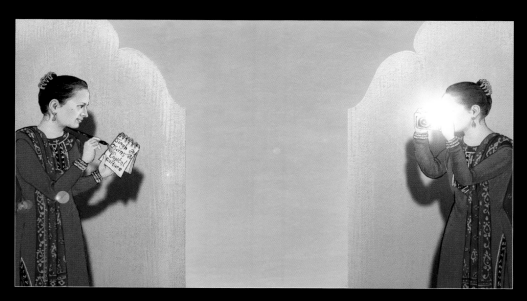

Some of the more obvious autobiographical references in the animation are where we appear ourselves both in painted form holding a camera and note pad and then in archive video footage working on the 'Liverpool 800' painting. These say something about our role as official documenters of our home city and, in that respect, our personal sense of accomplishment as artists who have contributed to the preservation of history and to contemporary British art through our public commissioned works and 'The Making of Liverpool'.

Left. Stills from The Singh Twins sequence in 'The Making of Liverpool' animation.
Right. Other stills from the animation showing The Singh Twins working on the 'Liverpool 800' painting.

Angela Heslop:

What about reaching new audiences with the film? It's been screened at the Liverpool Philharmonic Hall and film festivals. Were you hoping to reach a new audience for your painting then? Perhaps getting to people who wouldn't necessarily walk into an art gallery?

That was one of the key processes in our thinking, yes, because, as a public commission work, the painting itself is not readily available to exhibit outside Liverpool. But having it represented in a film, which you can potentially screen anywhere in the world, means it can be shared with a much wider audience.

Above. The Singh Twins with animators Andy, Mike and Neil, displaying the Creative Media Award which 'The Making of Liverpool' received at the Hollywood film festival.

Above. The animation's creative team Steve, Tom, Mike, Heidi, Andy, Neil, Mark and The Singh Twins at its official press launch. Photo courtesy Liverpool Echo and Daily Post. *Below*. At the 'Sikh Lens' festival, Hollywood. Photo, Jag Reyatt.

The Singh Twins with Sparkle Media's Creative Director Andy, at the Canadian premiere screening of 'The Making of Liverpool'.

Angela Heslop:

Now, the content of the film is I think incredibly rich, because it is reminding us not only of our historical heritage but culture and politics as well. Was the variety that you have put into the film very important to you?

Yes, because it's a reflection of an artwork that took six months to research and represents what we found to be most facinating about Liverpool's history and achievements. So the variety of content that appears in the film, as with the painting which inspired it, is very personal to us and, with a history spanning 800 years, necessarily rich in detail.

Of course, within the choices we made there were obvious things to include, such as The Beatles and football, without which no documentation of Liverpool would be complete. But we wanted to get away from the stereotype image and made a conscious decision to underplay these two aspects of the city's culture because we felt there was so much more to Liverpool. Instead we prioritised the more unusual or less talked-about facts like the historical trade links with Ireland and pioneering achievements in social welfare.

Overall the content fulfilled one of our main objectives: to present a chronological and balanced account of Liverpool's developing history and identity, from its merchant maritime past to its current status as a world-class city of leisure, tourism and culture.

Other Liverpool Paintings

Angela Heslop:

When did you start using or painting Liverpool?

Working on 'Liverpool 800'.

Quite early on actually, because we have always been interested in exploring issues around heritage and culture and, in particular, the duality of our own identity as British-born Asians, where the landscape and buildings associated with our home city and the Liverpool region came to symbolise the predominantly western environment we grew up in, whilst retaining a strong affiliation with our traditional Indian practices and values.

One of our first works to use the Liverpool cityscape as a symbol of the West and our connection with that side of our heritage was 'Wedding Jange II', which shows a traditional Indian wedding celebration on the banks of the River Mersey.

Another work from the same period as 'Wedding Jange II', entitled 'All That I Am', is a narrative portrait illustrating our father's life story, achievements and impact on our lives. This time Liverpool is represented by one of its most recognisable landmarks, the Liver Building. It is situated on a river next to Big Ben to create a fantasy cityscape symbolising a particular episode in his personal story of migration from India to Britain; the time he relocated the family from London to Liverpool to teach and read for medicine at Liverpool University, marking the beginning of our own connection with the city.

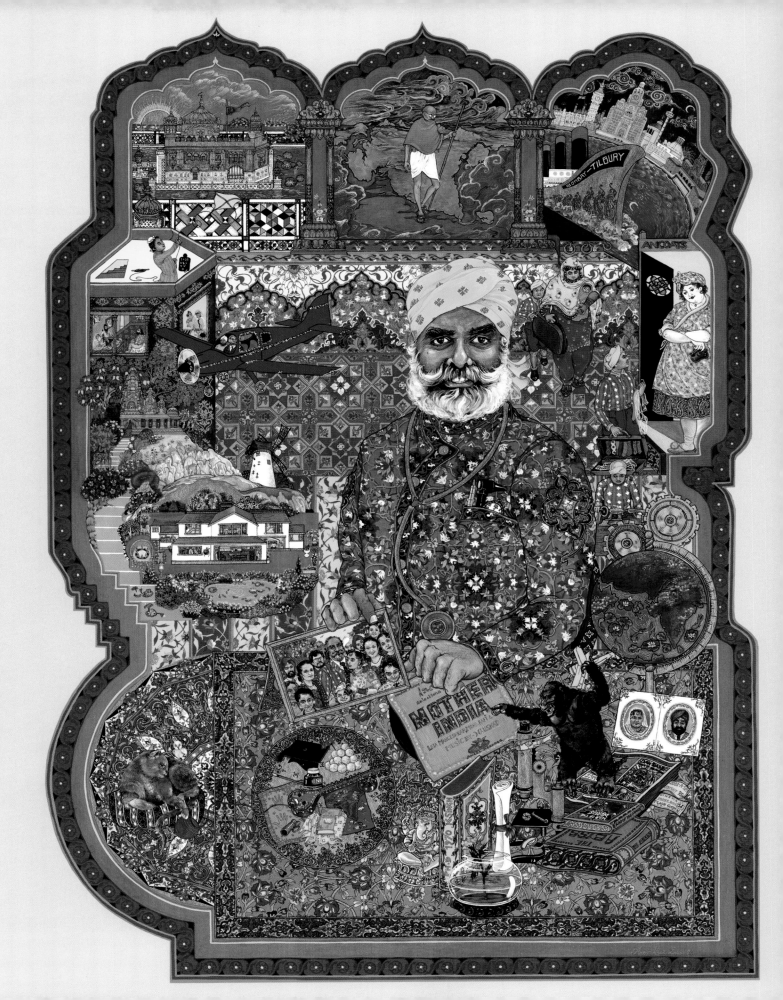

'Indian Summer at Dhigpal Nivas' is another celebration of our multicultural experience and similarly uses the Liverpool cityscape to locate the traditional Asian family enjoying a classically British pastime with an Indian twist, firmly on British soil.

'Painting the Town Red' and 'O come All Ye Re-eds', 1996

Moving away from images of our personal history and identity, many of the paintings we have subsequently created with a Liverpool reference were commissioned for other people. So in some ways they reflect the brief and specific interests of the client. 'Painting the Town Red' (left) and 'O Come All Ye Re-eds' (overleaf), for example, were both created for a London curator who had seen our work on show during our 1999 UK tour and invited us to produce works on the theme of football for an exhibition he was curating around the 1996 Euro Cup entitled 'England's Glory'.

Government Art Collection, UK.

Left. Detail from 'Painting the Town Red'.

We confess football was not something we were remotely interested in or inspired by, but we decided to rise to the challenge and found a way to explore the theme from a perspective that fitted in with issues we were exploring in our work at that time – looking at the game as a wider expression of Liverpool's multicultural, celebratory character and the religious-like status it has been given by fans and media alike.

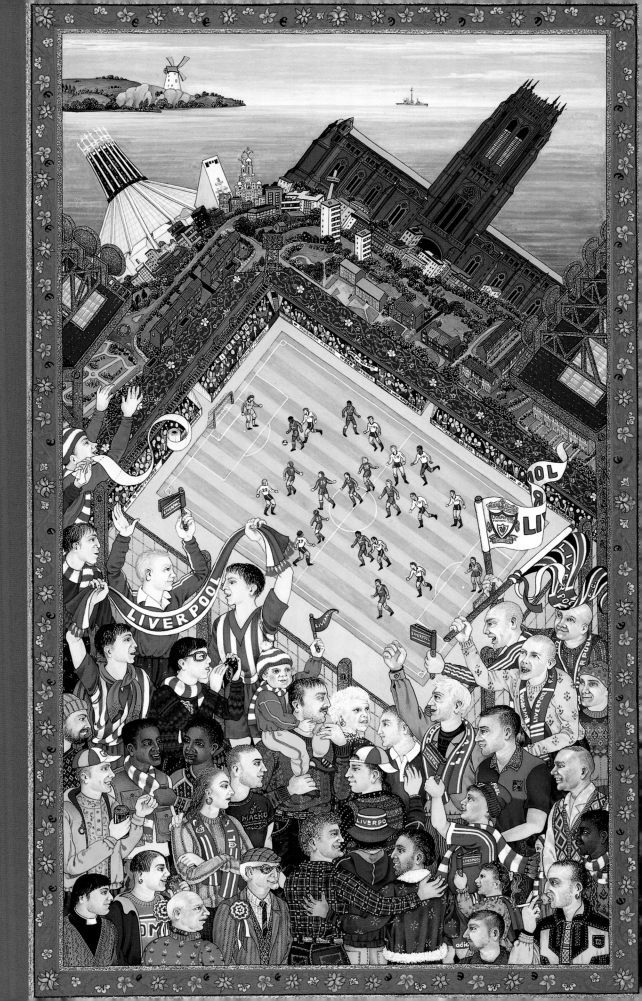

Right. 'O Come All Ye Re-eds'. National Museums Liverpool.

Private Collection, the Davies family.

'Fantasy Liverpool', 2006

'Fantasy Liverpool' is a private commission that focuses on an area of the city and specific buildings and artworks around the city which the clients especially connected with in some way. The work also documents something about their family history and cultural identity outside of Liverpool, such as their interest in India and personal links with Wales and the Wirral. So it's very much their vision of the city and its significance within their wider experience of life.

143

'The FACT Portraits', 2003

Billy Flynn.

Our first especially commissioned public artwork for Liverpool is the one we did for FACT (Foundation for Art and Cultural Technology). It's unusual in that it is more about the history of a building than the city itself, reflecting not only the various personalities, contribution and vision of those who were involved in its construction, but the collective aspirations for its future as a purpose-built creative centre serving and connecting artists and community groups.

Commissioned by the Foundation for Art and Creative Technology (FACT).

Roy Stringer.

Iassac Julian

Olga Bailey.

Jamie Scott.

Geoff Horsley.

Gina Grey.

'Manchester Reviewed', 2002

One of the public commissions we did as official artists-in-residence for the 2002 Manchester Commonwealth Games, 'Manchester Reviewed', uses popular imagery associated with well-known Liverpool tourist and festival attractions (the Beatles' 'Yellow Submarine' sculpture and a Tall Ship) to represent the city as one of several locations that share the stage with Manchester as key places of interest within the Northwest.

The Museum of London Collections.

'Entwined', 2010

One of our favourite works with a Liverpool reference is the commission we did for the Museum of London entitled 'Entwined', which responds to issues around the Indian Mutiny, or First War of Indian Independence as it is now known. In this painting both the Liverpool Liver Building and Town Hall come together with other buildings and monuments from cities around Britain to create an imaginary landscape, signifying where Asians have settled and how they have impacted on British society as a result of the relationship established between Britain and India during the Raj and its ongoing legacy.

Wider Themes...

Angela Heslop:

What about the themes in your paintings before Liverpool?

Liverpool has featured in our work since the beginning, but outside of this particular interest in our home city our themes have varied quite a bit. Ranging from explorations of personal and collective heritage and identity, to more overtly political subjects and topics around popular culture such as sport and celebrity. Commenting, for example, on issues of debate around genetic engineering, the commercialisation of sport, media representations of femininity and the state of relationships in our modern times.

...Influences and Motivation.

Angela Heslop:

Do you see your work as redefining cultural heritage and identity?

Yes we do, because from the outset it's been about challenging accepted notions of heritage and identity in reaction to what we have experienced as British Asians and, generally, as the negative attitudes towards traditional and non-western lifestyles and values, including the institutionalised prejudice we have had to battle against as contemporary artists heavily inspired by a traditional Indian art form.

Our work tries to counter what we feel are popular perceptions of 'West is best' and the tendency to separate East and West, tradition and modernity. Where traditional and eastern cultures are all too often regarded as being equally inferior and opposite to the West and modernity. As individuals born into cultures on both sides of the fence, many of our works in style and theme project our personal standpoint: that it shouldn't have to be about choosing between the two – as we felt pressured to do as young Asians growing up in Britain, by our peers and by negative media stereotypes of Asian culture – and that it is possible to celebrate

the best of both worlds without compromising your sense of personal identity. Within this context our work also looks at how culture is defined and evaluated – presenting dialogues around the origins of culture and demonstrating how, in reality, there are crossovers and historical links between us all which need to be understood and recognised more if we are to combat prejudice rooted in misplaced notions of cultural superiority and division.

Left. Detail of The Singh Twins' painting 'From Zero to Hero' (from the 'Sportlight Series') 2002. Depicting David and Victoria Beckham as they have been dubbed by the media, as the 'New Royal Family' and the king and queen of celebrity, representing the perfect union of the worlds of pop, fashion and sport.

A detail from 'Nyrmla's Wedding II'. The Singh Twins,1996.

All these issues are things that we express as personal opinions through our work, but which we feel strike a chord with many people for whom, in an increasingly global society, traditional values, practice and ideals are both important and relevant. In a modern world where westernisation is still generally regarded as synonymous with progress and civilisation, and where western culture continues to be elevated as the benchmark, or norm, for acceptance, we believe that art plays a key role in communicating ideas about heritage, identity and culture that invite people to reassess how they see themselves in relation to the 'other' and help break down cultural barriers. This is why such issues have dominated our work, regardless of the theme.

Angela Heslop:

Could you just talk a little bit about how your interest in the Indian miniature art form developed?

It all started on our first visit to India. Our father took us there as teenagers in 1980. It was also his first time back in 30 years after escaping to the UK as a small boy during the political turmoil of the Partition of India in 1947. The journey was a huge adventure because we didn't just go the 'normal' way. Our father and his brothers built a motor home and we drove from England through Europe, the Middle East (during the Iran–Iraq war) and into India, where we travelled around for nine months experiencing India in all its diversity. It was a significant turning point in our lives and left us with a deep sense of belonging and an emotional connection with India. As we travelled around monuments, temples, palaces and museums, we were bombarded with examples of India's rich artistic heritage. One of the things we came across was the Indian miniature tradition, whose exquisite beauty, remarkable detail and breathtaking technical skill just blew us away. We also visited some contemporary art galleries but were disappointed to find most of the artwork just aping western trends in art. There was very little indication of artists drawing upon traditional Indian art and it seemed to us that the miniature genre in particular had been totally rejected by India's contemporary art establishment. Which we felt was a great shame.

Above. Detail from 'Entwined', representing the vehicle in which The Singh Twins first travelled to India.

From that point onwards it became our mission to revive and develop the miniature to make it relevant to contemporary audiences and modern art practice. As teenagers we would visit museums in the UK and photograph Indian miniatures in close-up detail, then blow these up to see what brush techniques were used so we could try and emulate them. We started off by copying famous examples of historical miniatures and then applied the techniques we had learnt, first to producing modern reinterpretations of those historical works and then to creating our own themes in a modified version of the style which in part also drew on artistic conventions from other global traditions.

At university, our continued adoption of the miniature style became a political statement in itself when the art tutors dismissed it as "backward", "outdated" and "of no relevance to contemporary art". We were told instead to look to western role models for inspiration, and predominantly those who were being presented to us as the great innovators and fathers of modern art, such as Matisse, Gauguin and Picasso. This betrayed to us not only a double standard in our tutors' thinking, but a serious lack of appreciation and recognition of the impact of non-European art forms on the development of western art history, given that many of these artists had themselves looked to traditional art forms from Africa, Persia, India, Japan and Tahiti for inspiration and had championed the cause of artistic freedom and self-expression which was being denied to us.

Left. The Golden Temple Amritsar, and other examples of Indian art, which inspired and were photographed by The Twins whilst in India.

At the same time, whilst we ourselves recognised that these artists were innovators within their own cultural context and times, we didn't see why we should be forced, in effect, to accept their art and the movements they initiated as somehow superior. Because as far as we could see many of the artistic traits and forms of creative expression attributed to the trendsetters of modern art were already being employed centuries earlier in the diverse traditions of 'ethnic' arts, including India's classical and folk art. Several of the stylistic and compositional conventions that Matisse used, for example, are characteristic of Indian and Persian miniature painting: the way that he divided space; flattened perspective; adopted multi-perspective views; his use of pattern; symbolic colour and stylised and abstract form.

The dictates of our art tutors strengthened our resolve to develop the Indian miniature aesthetic through our own paintings as a way of challenging what we felt to be their unacceptable Eurocentric evaluation of art and asserting the validity of traditional and non-European art forms within modern art practice. Our determination to prove our point and justify our chosen path in art through academic research cost us our degree when an examiner refused to mark our final year dissertations, both of which focused on the significant impact of traditional non-European art forms on western art.

In terms of promoting our work within the mainstream, we have been confronted with similar attitudes of cultural bias. Within the gallery and museum world if curators have not rejected our work altogether, because they can't see its relevance to mainstream audiences, there has been a tendency to exhibit it only as part of a celebration of India or 'Indian season'. But just how ingrained this attitude of cultural selectivity is within society generally was brought home to us by a national televised art competition we entered as young students, when the programme's producers

publicly announced that whilst our work complied with all the judging criteria it was "too culturally different" to be considered alongside other entrants.

Above. A copy of Henri Matisse's 'La Dessert', 1908. This detail from The Singh Twins' painting, 'The Last Supper', 1995, makes a satirical commentary on the impact of non-European art on western art.

To some extent we have achieved success by having to make the most of certain opportunities presented to us by this 'ethnic pigeon holing' of our work, which by and large we have managed to do on our own terms – ensuring that our involvement also complies with and furthers our personal interests and objectives as artists. But it has to be said that we have also been very fortunate in our career to have had, and been able to build on, the support of other individuals within the arts who have genuinely appreciated the relevance of our work to contemporary artistic expression and global audiences.

Left above. 'Battle of The Giants (from the 'Sportlight Series').The Singh Twins, 2002. A contemporary reinterpretation of the elephant fight theme in Indian miniature painting.
Right. 'Love Lost'. The Singh Twins, 2000. Private Collection. A modern reworking of the traditional 'lovers' theme in Indian miniature painting.

more about the tremendously exciting technologies of moving imagery and creative digital media – so that we can push the boundaries of our own creativity, but also the modern development of the miniature, even further.

Angela Heslop:

Can I thank you Amrit and Rabindra for being absolutely fascinating. I have admired your work for a good number of years and watched it develop. And really, just to hear about the process of your animation film has been extraordinary. So thank you both very much.

Over a period of more than two decades we have come a long way with the Indian miniature. So, when people sometimes ask us when we are going to move on from it, we reply: "If something's not broken why try and fix it." Because we never cease to be amazed by this richly diverse and versatile genre of Indian art and have so much more yet to discover and be inspired by.

At the same time our exploration of film has opened up a whole new world of possibilities and our first animation, 'The Making of Liverpool', has definitely whet our appetite for wanting to learn

Left. Early studies of Indian miniature portraits by The Singh Twins.
Right. Portrait of The Singh Twins by Dan Kenyon. 2009. Collection National Portrait Gallery, London.

Artists' Profile

The Singh Twins are contemporary British artists of international standing, whose award-winning paintings have been acknowledged as constituting a unique genre in British art and for initiating a new movement in the revival of the Indian miniature tradition within modern art practice. Describing their work as 'Past Modern' (as opposed to Post Modern), they engage with important areas of critical debate, challenging existing stereotypes and redefining generally accepted, narrow perceptions of heritage and identity in art and society. Combining elements from western and eastern aesthetics they assert the value of traditional and non-European art forms to the continuing development of contemporary art practice – exploring cultural, social and political issues of global significance within a highly decorative, often witty and symbolic style which has universal appeal and transcends cultural barriers.

Exhibitions of paintings from the significant body of work they have created since 1987 have been hosted by museums and galleries around the world, including The National Gallery and National Portrait Gallery, London; The Walker Art Gallery, Liverpool; The Smithsonian Institution, Washington; The Royal Museums, Edinburgh; The Gallery of Modern Art, Glasgow; McMaster Gallery, Hamilton, Canada and The National Gallery of Modern Art, Mumbai and New Delhi, where they became the only British artists besides Henry Moore to have been offered a solo show at this, India's foremost venue for contemporary art.

Above. The Singh Twins as invited speakers at the Smithsonian Institution.
Right, top to bottom. The Singh Twins visiting their work in the National Gallery, London's Love exhibition.Book signing at the opening of their National Gallery of Modern Art, Mumbai, solo show. Filming for Open University.

With paintings in private and public collections worldwide, from The Royal Ontario Museum, Toronto to The Museum of London, the Twins continue to be invited to speak at institutions such as The Tate Gallery, London; The Art Gallery of Ontario, Canada; The National Gallery of Modern Art, Delhi and Mumbai; The Asian Art Museum, San Francisco and The Library of Congress, Washington.

During the past two decades their work has received significant interest from academics, art students and university research scholars alike and is incorporated into the formal education system of Britain and elsewhere.

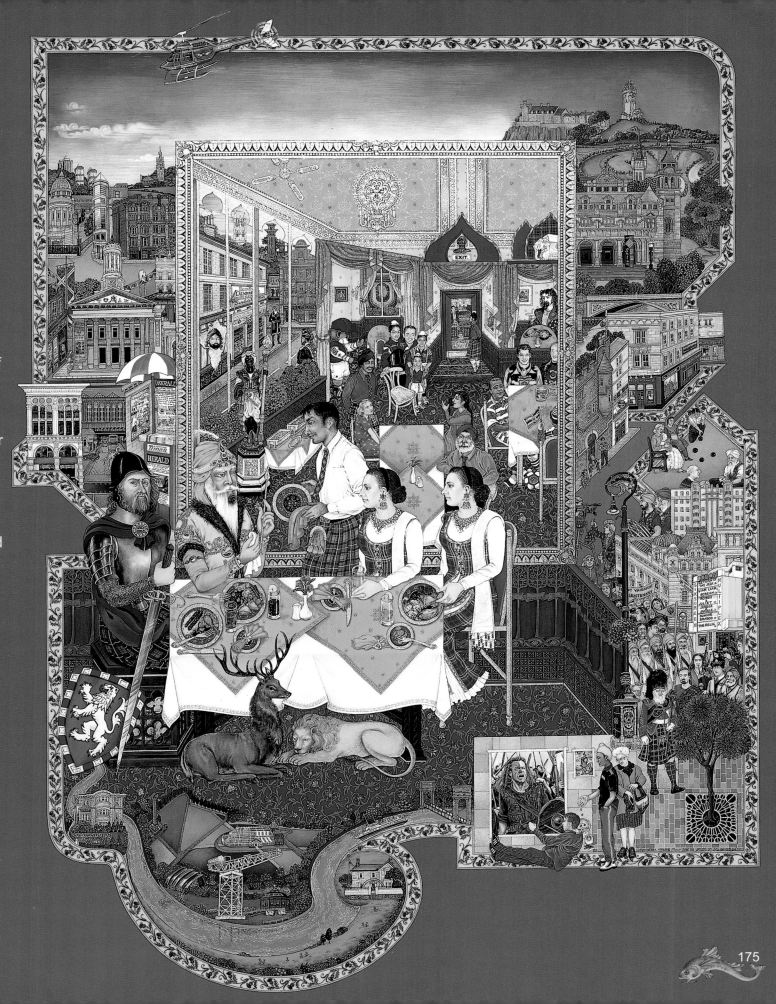

Right. 'Mr Singh's India'. The Singh Twins, 2000. Glasgow Museums commission. A painting about Scottish Sikh identity and shared heritage. Currently on display at the Kelvingrove Art Gallery and Museum.

175

ELLE NOW

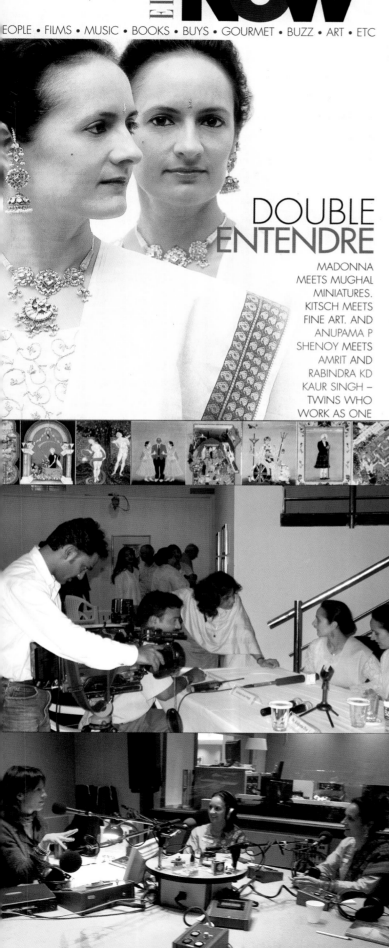

EOPLE • FILMS • MUSIC • BOOKS • BUYS • GOURMET • BUZZ • ART • ETC

DOUBLE ENTENDRE

MADONNA
MEETS MUGHAL
MINIATURES.
KITSCH MEETS
FINE ART. AND
ANUPAMA P
SHENOY MEETS
AMRIT AND
RABINDRA KD
KAUR SINGH –
TWINS WHO
WORK AS ONE

Their contribution to the arts has achieved wide media attention – featuring in numerous art magazines, journals and newspapers across the globe. Television and radio coverage has included house guest appearances on Bloomberg TV's 'Style', Carlton TV's 'Open House' with Gloria Hunniford and CBC's 'Here and Now', as well as interviews for BBC 'Women's Hour', 'Mid Week', 'Front Row' and 'Belief'. In 1998 a film entitled 'Singh Out Sisters' which followed their first exhibition in Germany was screened by Granada Television as part of a series of programmes profiling the creative talent of North West England and, in 2001, an Arts Council-funded documentary on their work by independent film maker Suman Bhuchar entitled 'Alone Together' received 'The Best Film on Art' prize at the Asolo International Film Festival.

That same year the Twins were shortlisted for the Asian Women of Achievement Awards (in the category of Arts & Culture) and in 2002 were appointed official Artists-in-Residence to the UK Manchester Commonwealth Games.

Amongst the mainstream publications profiling their work are such titles as 'The Penguin History of Scotland', 'The Oxford History of Art: Portraiture', the National Portrait Gallery's 'The Portrait Now', Marg Publications' 'New Insights into Sikh Art' and 'The Oxford Encyclopedia of Women in World History'.

Left top to bottom. The Singh Twins featured in Elle Magazine (Courtesy Elle), being interviewed for Indian television and as house guests of Avril Benoit on CBC radio's 'Here and Now'.

Other Interests

Although more widely known for their paintings, The Singh Twins are also published writers and authors. Publications include a children's poetry book entitled 'Bindhu's Weddings', inspired by their paintings of British Asian life, and an art history book, 'Images of Freedom', which draws on a selection of posters from the archive of popular and mass-produced imagery pertaining to India which they began collecting during their time as postgraduate students in 1990.

Further Information

THE SINGH TWINS

Other Fine Art publications and DVDs profiling The Singh Twins and their work include:

'Worlds A-part: Paintings by The Singh Twins'
ISBN 978-0-9535111-1-2
Published by Twin Studio

'Bindhu's Weddings'
Published by The Sikh Foundation, California

'Twin Perspectives: Paintings by Amrit and Rabindra KD Kaur Singh'
ISBN 978-0-9535111-0-5
Published by Twin Studio

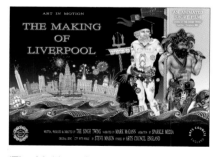

'The Making of Liverpool' DVD.
Supported by Liverpool City Council
www.playedinbritain.co.uk
www.liverpool.gov.uk and
Ian Freeman, Creative Director of
Moovie Productions Limited.

'Nineteen Eighty-Four and the Via Dolorosa Project' DVD
Supported by Sikhpoint.com

For full details of the above and other reproductions of The Singh Twins' work visit the 'Shop' page at www.singhtwins.co.uk.

MARK MCGANN

To find out more about Mark McGann, his educational and screen production work and his music visit:
www.mcgannbrothers.org.uk

www.dramadirect.net

www.screendirect.net

www.isound.com/mark_mcgann

SPARKLE MEDIA

To find out more about Sparkle's Visual Effects and Animation work visit:
www.sparklemedia.co.uk

STEVE MASON

To find out more about Steve Mason and his music visit:
www.myspace.com/stevemasonsongs

Picture Credits and Research Sources